ON THE ETERNITY
OF THE WORLD

JOHN PECHAM

QUESTIONS CONCERNING THE
ETERNITY OF THE WORLD

Translated by
VINCENT G. POTTER, S.J.

Fordham University Press
New York
1993

© Copyright 1993 Fordham University Press
All rights reserved

LC-93-26602

ISBN 0-8232-1488-5 (clothbound)

Library of Congress Cataloging-in-Publication Data

Peckham, John, d. 1292.
  (De aeternitate mundi. English & Latin)
  Questions concerning the eternity of the world / John Pecham;
translated by Vincent G. Potter.
     p.   cm.
  Includes bibliographical references.
  ISBN 0-8232-1488-5 : $25.00
  1. Cosmology–Early works to 1800. 2. Eternity–Early works to 1800.
3. Creation–Early works to 1800. 4. Infinity–Early works to 1800.
I. Potter, Vincent G. II. Title.
B765.P43D4313 1993
113–dc20
                                                          93-26602
                                                          CIP

The Latin text and notes and the description of the manuscripts are reproduced from Ignatius Brady, "John Pecham and the Background of Aquinas's *De aeternitate mundi*," in *St. Thomas Aquinas, 1274–1974: Commemorative Studies II,* ed. Armand A. Maurer, C.S.B., 2 vols. (Toronto: Pontifical Institute of Mediaeval Studies, 1974), pp. 155–78. Copyright © 1974 by the Pontifical Institute of Mediaeval Studies, Toronto.

Printed in the United States of America

CONTENTS

FOREWORD

The occasion for this translation of John Pecham's *De aeternitate mundi* was a graduate course which I taught some time ago on Aquinas' *opuscula*. Because Thomas' *On the Eternity of the World* was among those short works, I thought it would be useful if my students knew something of the differences of opinion on the matter current in the thirteenth century. Moreover, according to Ignatius Brady, it is very likely that Thomas' work was written in direct response to Pecham's. Although Thomas' essay was available in English, Pecham's was not, and it was unlikely that many of my graduate students could handle the original. Hence, a translation was needed.

I trust others may find Pecham's thesis about the world's "eternity" both interesting in itself and revelatory of the philosophical and theological controversies of thirteenth-century Europe.

I am indebted to the late Rev. George S. Glanzman, S.J., for reading an early version of my translation and for his helpful corrections, emendations, and suggestions. I am similarly indebted to Professor G. J. Etzkorn of the Franciscan Institute of St. Bonaventure University (St. Bonaventure, N.Y.) for reading the translation and offering further corrections and suggestions. Finally, I am grateful to Rev. Louis B. Pascoe, S.J., Professor of Medieval History, Fordham University, and to Rev. Brian Davies, O.P., Blackfriars, Oxford, for their help in preparing the introductory material dealing, respectively, with the ceremonies involved in a doctoral defense at the University of Paris in the days of St. Thomas, and with the Latin Averroist controversy at Paris in the thirteenth century. Whatever shortcomings remain are my own.

Introduction to John Pecham's
De aeternitate mundi

LIFE AND WORK

JOHN PECHAM, O.F.M., was born in about the year 1230 at Patcham, Sussex, England.[1] He studied at the faculty of arts in Paris and quite possibly was a pupil of Roger Bacon's. He completed his study of arts, however, at Oxford where he became acquainted with Adam Marsh (Adam de Marisco), the first Franciscan master in theology at that university, who probably influenced his decision to join the Franciscan Order. Most likely, however, he was already ordained a priest when he entered at Oxford and where he completed his novitiate. At some date between 1257 and 1259 he returned to Paris to begin his theological studies. In about 1269–1270 he became *magister theologiae* and lectured in theology at the Franciscan Friary in Paris until about 1271.

Pecham was in Paris at a very lively time. Two "innovations" were under attack: (1) the mendicant orders (Franciscans and Dominicans), founded during the first decade of the thirteenth century, and representing a radical departure from the monastic conception of religious life more or less standardized in the *Rule* of St. Benedict; these new religious groups were not confined to monasteries, but moved about preaching and teaching in a more active way than the contemplative monks; and (2) the "new" philosophy of Aristotle introduced into Paris from Muslim Andalusia. Out of these two innovations three controversies arose. The first involved the so-called Latin Averroists, or radical Aristotelians, who held some theses that were contrary to the Faith, such as the unicity of the intellect and the eternity of the world, in the sense that it was not created. Franciscans and Dominicans agreed in rejecting the Averroist point of view. The second controversy, however, was between the Dominicans and the Franciscans and involved the truth of certain other (*per se* orthodox) Aristotelian theses, such as the unicity of substantial form and the demonstrability of the world's having a beginning in time. The third controversy had to do with the legitimacy of the religious life as understood and practiced within these new religious Orders. This new way of life came under fierce attack by the secular clergy, and the controversy took an unseemly turn, often becoming vitriolic and *ad hominem* on both sides. Hence, Pecham witnessed Franciscans and Dominicans allied against the Averroists and again allied against the attacks of the secular clergy. Yet on the place of Aristotelianism in orthodox theology Pecham saw his Order opposed to the Dominicans. It was during this period that Pecham and Thomas met and probably had an encounter on the occasion of Pecham's "inception" ("doctoral defense").

Pecham left Paris for Oxford again in about 1272. There he became lector in theology at the Franciscan Friary and held this post until 1275 when he was made Provincial of his Order in England. During these three years of teaching Pecham became engaged in a rather bitter controversy with the Dominican Robert Kilwardby about the proper understanding of evangelical poverty as an apostolic virtue. Both orders, Franciscan and Dominican, were "mendicant," but they did not understand religious "poverty" in exactly the same way, and so how that poverty was to be lived out was a matter of dispute between them. Even within the Franciscan Order itself there were differences of opinion on the matter of evangelical poverty which eventually caused the Order itself to divide into various factions. This important and sensitive point had been, for a time, overshadowed by the attack of the secular clergy which had forced the two Orders to put aside their differences to make common cause against a mortal enemy. But once that danger was past, their differences surfaced again in a rather acrimonious way.

In 1277 Pecham was appointed by Pope John XXI to the lectorship in theology (*Lector sacri palatii*) at the papal Roman Curia (founded by Innocent IV). Pecham held the post for about two years, and it was a time of fruitful literary and academic work. Among his works of this period which have survived are a commentary on the Canticles, a *Quodlibet*, and a number of *Quaestiones* on such topics as the glorified body, the beatific vision, and others.[2] The fact that this post was always held by a Franciscan until the end of the thirteenth century testifies to the papal attitude of distrust toward the "new" philosophy and theology. Perhaps it was this papal disfavor which made possible the 1277 condemnations of certain Aristotelian theses both at Paris and at Oxford. Although these condemnations were aimed principally against the Averroists, Thomists were also affected since they were accused of supporting some of the condemned theses. In that same year at Oxford those theses were also condemned by the Archbishop of Canterbury, himself a Dominican, Robert Kilwardby.[3]

On the feast of the Conversion of St. Paul in 1279, Pecham was named Archbishop of Canterbury by Pope Nicholas III, presumably to accomplish the ecclesial reforms mandated by the second Council of Lyons which his predecessor, the Dominican Kilwardby, had failed to do.

In 1286, Kilwardby's condemnation of 1277 was renewed by John Pecham. Pecham's personal convictions in this matter are clearly stated in a letter of his to the bishop of Lincoln, June 1, 1285:

"I do not in any way disapprove of philosophical studies, insofar as they serve theological mysteries, but I do disapprove of irreverent innovations in language, introduced within the last twenty years into the depths of theology against philosophical truth, and to the detriment of the Fathers, whose positions are disdained and openly held in contempt. Which doctrine is more solid and more sound, the doctrine of the sons of St. Francis . . . or that very recent and almost entirely contrary doctrine, which fills the entire world with wordy quarrels, weakening and destroying with all its strength what Augustine teaches concerning the eternal rules and the unchangeable light, the faculties of the soul, the seminal reasons included in matter and innumerable questions of the same kind; let the Ancients be the judges, since in them is wisdom; let the God of heaven be judge, and may He remedy it."[4]

There is no doubt that Pecham is referring to Dominican Aristotelianism. Evidently, then, the Roman Curia during this period sided with the "traditional" Augustinianism of the Franciscans rather than with the "new theology." Pecham was at once against the Averroists and against the Thomists. He opposed the Averroists, for example, in their denial of divine providence, and he opposed the Thomists, for example, on the unicity of substantial form. With respect to the "eternity" of the world, both Pecham and Thomas opposed the Averroists but in different ways, as we shall see.

Pecham died on December 8, 1291, no doubt disappointed that the reform movement for which he had been appointed never came to pass.

THE LATIN AVERROISTS

The term "Averroism"[5] has been commonly associated with a form of thirteenth-century "integral" or "radical" Aristotelianism, as Copleston calls it.[6] The term comes from "Averroës," the Latinized form of the name of Ibn Rashd (1126–1198), known as the "Commentator" because of his extensive work on Aristotle.

Perhaps the best-known Averroist was Siger of Brabant (ca. 1235–1282), who taught in the faculty of arts at Paris. The doctrines of the Averroists principally responsible for the movement's being condemned as heretical were: (1) the unicity of the intellect in mankind, and (2) the eternity of the world. The first position held that not only the active but also the passive intellect is "separate" from the human soul and indeed is one and the same for all humans. This is an interpretation of an obscure passage in Aristotle's De anima, III, 5. If the Averroists' version were followed, one consequence would be that there is no personal survival after death. The second Averroist position held that the "eternity" of the world is *demonstrable* by reason alone. By "eternity" was meant more precisely that the world had no beginning and/or no end and hence it can be demonstrated that there is no first or last member of the temporal series. As we shall see, such a series is more properly called "sempiternal," and failure clearly to distinguish the eternal from the sempiternal gave rise to much of the problem. If the Latin Averroists were right, there seemed to many Christians to be a conflict between what the faith teaches and what reason demands and so a choice between them would have to be made. Otherwise one would have to hold a doctrine of "two truths," a doctrine which Averroës and his Latin followers were accused of holding.

Both Franciscan and Dominican theologians rejected the Averroist position on the world's eternity but for rather different reasons. To understand the issues in this three-sided debate, it would be well to recall some of the basic tenets of "radical" or "integral" Aristotelianism. First, the Latin Averroists assumed (with Aristotle and all the ancient Greeks) that whatever is, always was, and always will be is *necessary*, that is, *not contingent*. Second, they held as self-evident the principle "From nothing, nothing comes," understood in the sense that every coming-to-be requires a material cause and so generation is the only conceivable kind of coming-to-be. Hence, if the world ever is, it always was and always will be. If there ever is any coming-to-be, there must be an infinity of comings-to-be *a parte ante* and *post*. The upshot of these two assumptions is that the world is ontologically necessary, hence non-contingent, hence not at all created in the orthodox Christian sense.

At the time of Pecham all Christians agreed that God alone is eternal, because as infinite, simple, and immutable, He transcends the temporal order. God is "beyond" or "outside of" time. They all further agreed that from this it follows that God had no beginning and will have no end; that God is, always was, and always will be. Hence in a sense God can be thought of as sempiternal (because eternal). All agreed, then, that this inference is valid:

If X is eternal, X is sempiternal.

Not all, however, agreed that the converse is valid:

If X is sempiternal, X is eternal.

This latter inference would be valid if and only if eternal and sempiternal were equivalent terms (as the radical Aristotelians assumed).

It may well be the case that the difference between the Franciscan and the Dominican rebuttals of the Latin Averroists' doctrine of the world's eternity has its origin in the Christian theological tradition up to the thirteenth century, which failed to make it sufficiently clear that these terms *are not* equivalent. If that had been made unmistakably clear, it would have been clear that to keep the world finite and contingent and God alone infinite and necessary, one does not have to demonstrate that the world is not sempiternal, that is, that the world has a first member in its temporal series. If sempiternal and eternal are assumed to be equivalent, sempiternity must be denied of a finite and contingent world.

It is interesting to note that most early versions of the cosmological argument attempt to demonstrate that the world had to have a beginning in time since it was argued that an infinite regress in causes is impossible.

If, then, one were to recognize that these terms are not equivalent, then all that would be required to reject the Latin Averroists' position on the world's eternity would be to show that it cannot be demonstrated by reason, and so if indeed the world had no beginning, that would be a matter of contingent fact and not a matter of necessary fact.

The Latin Averroists, as radical or integral Aristotelians, held that it *can be demonstrated* that the world *had no beginning* and will have no end. The Franciscans adopted the *contrary* position to the Averroists: namely, that it *can be demonstrated* that the world *had a beginning* (and perhaps also an end). The Dominicans adopted the *contradictory* position to the Averroists: namely, that it *cannot be demonstrated* that the world had no beginning. They also contradicted the Franciscans in that they denied one could demonstrate that the world had a beginning. Contrary positions cannot simultaneously be true but they may simultaneously be false. Hence it is possible that both the Averroists and the Franciscans were wrong. Contradictory positions can be neither simultaneously true, nor simultaneously false. If one is true, the other is false. Hence if the Dominican position is right, both the Averroists and the Franciscans are indeed mistaken (but, of course, for different reasons). Thomas Aquinas held that neither the "eternity" nor the "non-eternity" of the world is demonstrable by reason alone. Thomas was convinced that faith required Christians to hold that *in fact* the world is not eternal, but this comes solely from faith and not from reason. It cannot be demonstrated from reason either that the world is from eternity or that the world had a beginning. To deny either does not entail a contradiction. Hence each is at least logically possible. Only God can tell us which of these alternatives He freely chose for creation.

THE THOMISTS (DOMINICANS)

Concerning the eternity of the world, therefore, St. Thomas and the Dominicans, along with St. Bonaventure and the Franciscans, held that revelation teaches creation in time.[7] The *locus classicus* for this position is the text of the Fourth Lateran Council (November 30, 1215) which, against the Albigensian heresy, defined as belonging to the Christian Faith that God alone has no beginning but always is and always will be; that the eternal God is the one and only principle of all things, "creator of all things visible and invisible, spiritual and corporeal; by His almighty power, at the beginning of time He created both orders of creation alike out of nothing, the spiritual and the corporeal world, the angelic and the material."[8] Thomas, however, denied that it could be demonstrated by reason alone that this creation had a "beginning" in the sense of a first member of the temporal series. Hence God *could* (but *need not*) *have* created the world from eternity; in fact, He did not. There is nothing contradictory in supposing that God freely might have chosen to exercise His eternal power of creating from all eternity and that the world be nonetheless finite in the sense of totally dependent on God. We in the twentieth century, of course, might point to number theory for examples to serve as analogues. In essence, then, all that is required for the world to be created from nothing by a free act of divine choice is that it be totally dependent in its being upon God's creating and conserving power. This need not imply a first member of a series of spatio-temporal things (although Aquinas indeed believed that there *was* in fact such a member). Since pure creation is not change in the proper sense at all, it does not require that a potential principle be actualized as in the case of generation and corruption. Creation is not making something out of "nothing" or nonbeing where non-being is taken to be a material cause. Such a mistake is prompted perhaps by imagination but is not required by reason. Nor is it necessary that God exist "before" His effects because this supposes that God is somehow in time and subject to the conditions of temporal causes. All that reason requires is that God have the ontological priority of existing *a se*, absolutely independent of anything else and upon Whom all else depends for existence.

Aquinas treats the question of the world's eternity not only in the *opusculum* of that name, but also (to mention the most important places) in the *Summa contra Gentiles*, Book II, chaps. 31-38; in the *De potentia Dei*, q. 3, art. 17; and in the *Summa theologiae*, I, q. 46, art. 1 and 2.

THE BONAVENTURIANS (FRANCISCANS)

Bonaventure opposed the heretical theses of the Averroists, but did so along more traditional, "Augustinian" (hence, Neoplatonic) lines.[9] Thus, Bonaventure rejected the unicity of the intellect for all men but only in terms of a plurality of substantial forms in each man. Thomas too rejected the unicity of the intellect for all men but held for the unicity of substantial form in each man. Again, Bonaventure rejected the eternity of the world but held that the world's having been created in time (that is, having had a beginning) could be demonstrated. He was convinced that to prove eternal motion to be self-contradictory is to prove creation. Some of the standard arguments were: (1) the infinite cannot be traversed; (2) the infinite cannot be added to; (3) there cannot actually exist an infinite number of anything (usually put in terms of souls); (4) an infinite regress is impossible because it would exclude order (and God's providence), since an ordering supposes a first; and (5) if the world is created from nothing, it has its being after non-being and hence cannot be eternal.

Pecham's position is very much like Bonaventure's, except perhaps that his language is more Aristotelian. During Thomas' second regency at Paris, Pecham seems to have been the spokesman for a group that claimed that their view of creation was continuous with a tradition of orthodoxy going back to Augustine, particularly in *De civitate Dei* XII and in *Super Genesim* VIII. Following Bonaventure, then, Pecham maintained that the world *could not* be eternal and that reason can demonstrate that God existed "before" creation. Thus he denies Aquinas' position which admits the *possibility* of a created universe co-existing with God from all eternity. Those notions—creation and existing from eternity—are for Pecham incompatible. His basic reason for so thinking is that a created universe by its very nature is mutable, but nothing mutable can be co-eternal with the immutable God.

HISTORICAL CIRCUMSTANCES

Pecham's text, *De aeternitate mundi*, is in *quaestio* form.[10] A question is formulated; an answer (affirmative or negative) is declared; arguments against or objections to that answer are proposed; arguments are then offered in support of the proposed answer; and finally each objection is answered in turn. This format was very common and was used, for example, by Aquinas in the *Summa theologiae*. Ignatius Brady has argued convincingly that Thomas' *De aeternitate mundi* was written not against the Averroists as is usually assumed but rather against a presentation made by Pecham at his *inceptio* around 1270.[11]

The ceremony of inception in the Middle Ages marked a student's becoming a *magister regens*, that is, a regular member of the faculty. It included what is roughly equivalent to our doctoral thesis defense and an installation ceremony wherein the candidate was invested with the emblems of that office (ring and biretta—today: hood, cap, and gown). Palemon Glorieux points out that although we have no full account of how this ceremony was conducted in Paris, we do have such an account of it at Bologna.[12] He thinks it is likely that, despite regional variations, the ceremony was substantially the same throughout the European university community.

The ceremony lasted at least two days during which all classes and other academic exercises were suspended. All the masters and bachelors, as well as others, attended. A week or two before the ceremony the candidate for promotion to the "doctorate" circulated among all the masters and bachelors the questions (four in all, one for each session) to be discussed at the two sets of sessions which were to make up the ceremony, namely, two on the first day called the "vesperies" and two on the following day called the "aulica" (because they were held in the bishop's hall or *aula*).

The vesperies, as the name implies, were held in the afternoon of the first day, and the first two questions were taken up. The first session featured the bachelors, handling the first question, and was merely a warm-up for the second session (the vesperies proper), presided over by the candidate's thesis director (*magister aulator*), at which the new master (*magister aulandus*) bore the burden of disputing the second question. Who entered into this disputation with the candidate, in what capacity, and when during the proceedings were usually carefully defined by local custom. The details need not detain us.

On the following day the second session or "aulica" was held in the great hall of the bishop (at Paris anyway) and again was broken into two sessions: (1) the *disputatio in aula* which usually dealt with the third question and was again handled by the bachelors (now by those called "formed"), and (2) the *quaestio magistrorum* which took up the fourth and final question. This second session involved four masters disputing the issue in pairs. This discussion, however, came to an end deliberately without any definite conclusion being reached. The new master concluded this session by stating briefly his personal position concerning the third question discussed by the "formed" bachelors. After that there was a party for which the candidate paid!

Still this was not the end of the ceremony. There was one more session, held the next day or perhaps later, in which the new master was expected to fill in whatever was left incomplete or uncertain in the previous disputations and to settle "definitively" the third (and the fourth?) question which had been left rather up in the air. Hence, this part was called the *resumptio*. It took all morning and was the only item on the agenda. The master was expected to make a comprehensive presentation (*determinatio prolixa*). This seems to be what we have in the Pecham text herein translated. It seems that it is this *resumptio* which Thomas attacks in his own short piece on the world's eternity, and that Thomas himself had been present at Pecham's inception.

Weisheipl, in his biography of Aquinas, cites a story recounted by William of Tocco in his *Hystoria* which was meant to show Thomas' humility and learning: At the inception of a certain religious (unnamed), the young candidate took a position contrary to Thomas' (topic unspecified). On the way home some of Thomas' students were indignant that this young master should have challenged their professor and were upset that Thomas let the matter pass. Thomas explained that he did not wish to embarrass the young man, but if they thought the matter required it, he would intervene at the next day's session. The story goes that Thomas did so intervene and forced the young master to acknowledge his error. This could be a reference, thinks Weisheipl, to Pecham's *inceptio*.[13]

NOTES

1. For a life of Pecham, see D. L. Douie, *Archbishop Pecham* (Oxford: Clarendon, 1952).
2. Ibid., pp. 43–45.
3. See D. A. Callus, *The Condemnation of St. Thomas at Oxford*, Aquinas Papers 5 (Oxford: Blackfriars, 1946).
4. *Registrum epistolarum Fr. Johannis Pecham* III, ed. C. T. Martin (London, 1885), pp. 871, 901–902, cited by E. Gilson, *History of Christian Philosophy in the Middle Ages* (New York: Random House, 1955), p. 359, and in J. A. Weisheipl, O.P., *Friar Thomas d'Aquino: His Life, Thought, and Work* (Garden City, N.Y.: Doubleday, 1974), p. 288.
5. See P. F. Mandonnet, *Siger de Brabant et l'averroisme latin au XIIIe siècle*, 2 vols., 2nd ed., Les philosophes belges 6–7 (Louvain: Institut supérior de philosophie de l'Université, 1908, 1911); see also F. Copleston, S.J., *A History of Philosophy*. II. *Mediaeval Philosophy: Augustine to Scotus* (Westminster, Md.: Newman, 1955), pp. 435–41; Gilson, *Christian Philosophy*, pp. 387–405; for a version of Siger of Brabant different from Gilson's, see F. Van Steenberghen, *Siger de Brabant d'après ses oeuvres inédites*. II. *Siger dans l'histoire de l'Aristotélisme* (Louvain: Institut supérior de philosophie de l'Université, 1942) reproduced in part as *Aristotle in the West*, trans. L. Johnston (Louvain: Nauwelaerts, 1955).
6. Copleston, *History of Philosophy* II, p. 435.
7. For an authoritative biography of Aquinas see Weisheipl's *Friar Thomas d'Aquino*. See also Gilson's *Christian Philosophy*, pp. 361–83, 387–402, and Copleston's *History of Philosophy* II, pp. 423–34.
8. See H. Denzinger and A. Schonmetzer, S.J., *Enchiridion Symbolorum*, 33rd ed. (New York: Herder, 1965), No. 800.
9. See E. Gilson, *The Philosophy of St. Bonaventure* (New York: Sheed & Ward, 1938); Gilson, *Christian Philosophy*, pp. 327–61; Copleston, *History of Philosophy* II, pp. 240–92.
10. Ignatius Brady, O.F.M., "John Pecham and the Background of Aquinas's *De aeternitate mundi*," *St. Thomas Aquinas, 1274–1974: Commemorative Studies*, ed. Armand A. Maurer, C.S.B., 2 vols. (Toronto: Pontifical Institute of Mediaeval Studies, 1974), pp., 141–54; see also Weisheipl, *Friar Thomas d'Aquino*, pp. 287–90.
11. Brady, *art. cit.*
12. For a thorough study of the ceremony of inception see his "L'Enseignement au moyen âge: Techniques et méthodes en usage à la Faculté de Théologie de Paris au XIIIe siècle," *Archives d'histoire doctrinale et littéraire au moyen âge*, 35 (1968), 141–47.
13. Weisheipl, *Friar Thomas d'Aquino*, pp. 187–88. Among the selections from Aquinas in *On the Eternity of the World* (Thomas Aquinas, Siger of Brabant, and St. Bonaventure, *On the Eternity of the World (De aeternitate mundi)*, trans. C. Vollert, S.J., L. H. Kendzierski, and P. M. Byrne [Milwaukee: Marquette University Press, 1964]) is the treatise probably intended as an answer to Pecham.

SELECTED BIBLIOGRAPHY

Brady, I., O.F.M. "John Pecham and the Background of Aquinas's *De aeternitate mundi*." In *St. Thomas Aquinas, 1274–1974*: *Commemorative Studies*. Ed. Armand A. Maurer, C.S.B. 2 vols. Toronto: Pontifical Institute of Mediaeval Studies, 1974. II, Pp. 141–54.

Callus, D. A. *The Condemnation of St. Thomas at Oxford*. Aquinas Papers 5. Oxford: Blackfriars, 1946.

Copleston, F., S.J. *A History of Philosophy*. II. *Mediaeval Philosophy: Augustine to Scotus*. Westminster, Md.: Newman, 1955.

Douie, D. L. *Archbishop Pecham*. Oxford: Clarendon, 1952.

Gilson, E. *History of Christian Philosophy in the Middle Ages*. New York: Random House, 1955.

——. *The Philosophy of St. Bonaventure*. New York: Sheed & Ward, 1938.

Glorieux, P. "L'Enseignement au moyen âge: Techniques et méthodes en usage à la Faculté de Théologie de Paris au XIIIe siècle," *Archives d'histoire doctrinale et littéraire au moyen âge*, 35 (1968), 141–47.

Mandonnet, P. F., O.P. *Siger de Brabant et l'averroisme latin au XIIIe siècle*. 2 vols. 2nd ed. Les philosophes belges 6–7. Louvain: Institut supérior de philosophie de l'Université, 1908, 1911.

Steenberghen, F. van. *Siger de Brabant d'après ses oeuvres inédites*. II. *Siger dans l'histoire de l'Aristotélisme*. Louvain: Institut supérior de philosophie de l'Université, 1942. Reproduced in part as *Aristotle in the West*, trans. L. Johnston. Louvain: Nauwelaerts, 1955.

Thomas Aquinas, Siger of Brabant, and Bonaventure. *On the Eternity of the World (De aeternitate mundi)*. Trans. C. Vollert, S.J., L. H. Kendzierski, and P. M. Byrne. Milwaukee: Marquette University Press, 1964.

Weisheipl, J. *Friar Thomas d'Aquino: His Life, Thought, and Work*. New York: Doubleday, 1974.

A Note on the Text

Ignatius Brady, O.F.M.

The first Question of Pecham is taken from the only known manuscript, Florence Biblioteca Nazionale, *Conv. soppr.* J.I.3, ff. 59c–61a [= **F**].* The second Question is based on the same codex, ff. 61c–63a, and on a second, Florence Bibl. Medicea Laurenziana, *Santa Croce PL. XVII sin.* 8, ff. 97a–99c [= **L**]. I have not found any other manuscript.

F is well known as devoted wholly to the works of John Pecham, and has been described more than once. Cf. F. Tocco, in *Fratris Johannis Pecham Tractatus tres de paupertate* (British Soc. of Franc. Studies II, Aberdeen 1910) 99–108; H. Spettmann, *Johannis Pechami Quaestiones tractantes de anima* (Beiträge zur Gesch. der Phil. u. Theol. des Mittel. 19, Heft 5–6; Münster 1918), xxii–xxvii. For our Questions the text is very defective, with many lacunae (some of several lines in length), poor readings (as is evident from the text of some authorities cited), few corrections (errors are often marked with a cross in the margin, and sometimes by a cross over the word, but are not corrected; a later reader apparently had no other copy from which to correct the text). At the end, as also in codex **L**, the second question stops after the response to the eleventh objection.

L contains several works of Pecham; yet the present (second) Question is somehow included in a series of Questions that otherwise are to be attributed, at least in part, to Bartholomew of Bologna. See V. Doucet, "Notulae bibliographicae de quibusdam operibus Fr. Joannis Pecham, O.F.M.," *Antonianum* 8 (1933), 309–328; and M. Mückshoff, *Die Quaestiones disputatae De fide des Bartholomäus von Bologna, O.F.M.* (Beiträge 24, Heft 4; Münster, 1940), xxxiii–xxxv, and xliv. The text is, as a whole, of greater accuracy than that of **F**, and thus serves to correct the latter in many difficult passages.

It is quite evident, however, that there is no immediate or direct relationship between the two manuscripts. Both are almost assuredly of Parisian provenance; but **F** seems more likely to be the work of a student close to Pecham's term as *magister regens*, whereas **L** is later, at least after the regency of Bartholomew (ca. 1275–1277).

We should likewise note that Pecham's question in his commentary on the Sentences I, dist. 44, q. 3: *Quaeritur si potuit creare mundum antiquiorem* (cod. Florent., Bibl. Naz. *Conv. soppr.* G.4.854, f. 121c) is of no help either doctrinally or textually. — I am grateful to Dr. G. J. Etzkorn for making the original transcription from codex **F** of the two Questions published here; the text has since been critically compared to the manuscript itself.

Johannis Pechami
Quaestiones de aeternitate
mundi

I

Quaeritur utrum aliquid factum sit vel fieri potuit de nihilo ordinaliter.[1]

Et ostenditur quod non.

1. Quia teste Hieronymo:[2] "Cum Deus omnia possit, non potest tamen corruptam facere virginem." Sed maior est convenientia entis ad ens quam non-entis ad ens. Si igitur non potest Deus de corrupta facere virginem ordinaliter, multo magis nec de non-ente ens. — Respondebatur quod corruptio transit in praeteritum et non potest esse idem praeteritum et non praeteritum: ideo de corrupta non potest facere virginem.

2. Contra: eodem modo non-esse creaturae transit in praeteritum; ergo eadem ratione ei non potest succedere esse.

3. Item, maior est convenientia Creatoris cum creatura quam non-entis cum creatura, cum inter Creatorem et creatura sit analogia entis. Sed Deus non potest facere de Creatore creaturam, cum Creator sit immutabilis et creatura mutabilis. Ergo multo magis non potest facere de nihilo esse quod nullo modo convenit cum eo.

4. Item, si potest facere de non-ente ens, ergo cum infinita sit distantia non-entis ad ens, infinita distantia potest pertransiri.[3] Quod est falsum, quia secundum Philosophum:[4] "Infinitum non potest pertransiri nec a finito nec ab infinito."

---

[1] de nihilo *apparently deleted*; in the list of questions provided in **F** [f.19c], the title reads: *Utrum aliquid sit factum de nichilo ordinabiliter.*

[2] Epist. 22 (*ad Eustochium*), n. 5 (PL 22, 397; CSEL 54, 150). Cf. St. Thomas, *Summa theologiae* I, 25, 4, sed contra (ed. Ottawa 175a 43–45).

[3] Cf. St. Thomas, *Summa theol.* I, 45, 2, arg. 4 (284b 53–285a 2).

[4] Aristotle, *Post Anal.* I, 3(72b 10–11); and more directly, *Metaph.* X (XI), 10 (1066a 35–1066b 1).

John Pecham
Questions Concerning the Eternity of the World

I

The question is whether anything has been or could have been made out of nothing successively.

It is shown that the answer is negative.

1. Because, as Jerome witnesses, "Although God can do all things, still He cannot make a corrupted woman a virgin." But the affinity of being to being is greater than the affinity of non-being to being. If, therefore, God cannot make a virgin out of a corrupted woman successively, still less can He make being out of non-being. To this it was answered that the woman's fall passes into history and since the same thing cannot be both past and not past, therefore a virgin cannot be made out of a corrupted woman.

2. To the contrary: in like manner the *non-esse* of a creature passes into history, and so for the same reason *esse* cannot follow upon it.

3. Furthermore, there is a greater affinity between Creator and creature than between non-being and creature because between Creator and creature there is an analogy of being. But God cannot make a creature out of the Creator, since the Creator is immutable while the creature is subject to change. Still less, therefore, can *esse* be made out of nothing since *esse* has no affinity at all to it.

4. Again, if being can be made out of non-being, then since the distance from non-being to being is infinite, an infinite distance can be traversed. But this is false, since, according to the Philosopher: "An infinite expanse cannot be traversed either by a finite or by an infinite being."

5. Item, si potest super hanc distantiam quae est infinita, eadem ratione poterit super quamcumque aliam. Ergo potest inter distantiam quae est inter Creatorem et creaturam, cum una distantia infinita sit maior alia.

6. Item, omnis actio est per contactum vel corporalem ut in corporalibus, vel virtualem ut in spiritualibus. Si igitur Deus producit creatum [per] contactum virtutis suae: aut creatum prius est quam tangatur (dico 'prius' naturaliter), aut prius tangitur quam sit. Si primo modo: sed prius non causatur a posteriori; ergo creatura non creatur a contactu divinae virtutis. Si autem prius tangitur quam sit, contra: omne verbum includit in suo intellectu esse et addit super ipsum, secundum grammaticos. Unde sequitur: tangit, ergo est tangens; et tangitur, ergo est tactum. Si igitur prius est simplex quam compositum, et posterius est quod est ex additione ad alterum, prius est esse quam tangi, et ita ut supra: ipsum esse non creatur a contactu divinae virtutis.

7. Item, si creatura incepit esse, accipiamus instans quo incepit esse, et sit A. Item, si creatura prius habuit non-esse, accipiamus aliquod instans in quo non fuit, et sit B. Ergo inter A et B, cum se habeant secundum prius et prius, fuit tempus. Si dicas quod illud 'prius' fuit nunc aeternitatis,

8. Contra: ergo inceptio temporis fuit post aeternitatem vel nunc aeternitatis. Sed hoc est falsum, quia nunc aeternitatis omnia complectitur tempora; ergo etc.

9. Item, Deus secundum immensitatem essentiae comparatur ad mundi magnitudinem; secundum comparationem suae aeternitatis vel durationis comparatur ad mundi durationem. Sed, quamvis sit infinitas [= infinitus] magnitudine et mundus finitus, non tamen est extra mundum; ergo quamvis sit [in]finitus[5] aeternitate, non tamen fuit ante mundum.

---

[5] A cross is found in the margin, indicating either an error or an omission.

5. Further, if one has power over the infinite distance mentioned above, then for the same reason one would have power over any other distance. One would, therefore, have power over the distance between Creator and creature since the one infinite distance is greater than the other.

6. Again, every *actio* is by contact, either by bodily contact as in the case of physical things, or by virtual contact as in the case of spiritual beings. If, therefore, God produces what was created through His virtual contact, then either what was created exists before it is touched (I use "before" in its natural meaning) or else it is touched before it exists. If by the first alternative, then what already is is not caused by what comes after. The creature, then, is not caused by divine virtual contact. If, however, it is touched before it exists, one argues to the contrary: every verb, according to the grammarians, includes in its meaning "*esse*" and adds something to it. Whence it follows: "it touches" means "it is touching," and "it is touched" means "it is" plus "touched." If, therefore, the simple is prior to the composite, and if what is added on to another is posterior, then "to be" is prior to "to be touched" and so on as above: *esse* itself, then, is not created by divine virtual contact.

7. Further, suppose a creature began to be; then let us take the instant in which it began to be; call it A. Again, suppose that at a prior time a creature had *non-esse*; then let us take some instant in which it was not; call it B. Between A and B, then, since they are related as "before" and "before," there was time. If you should say that this "before" was the now of eternity,

8. then, to the contrary, it is argued: it follows, therefore, that the beginning of time was after eternity or the now of eternity. But this is false, since the now of eternity embraces all time: therefore, etc.

9. Again, the immensity of God's essence is compared to the magnitude of the world: God's eternity or duration is compared to the duration of the world. But, although God is infinite in extent and the world is finite, still He is not outside of the world; consequently, even though God's eternity is infinite, still He was not before the world.

10. Item, si non-esse praecedit esse: aut prioritate naturae, et hoc non, quia nihil non dicit naturam, ergo nec ordinem naturae; aut prioritate temporis, et hoc non, quia tempus prius non fuit; aut aeternitatis, et hoc non, quia aeternitas Dei est ipse Deus. Sed ipsum nihil non est in Deo, ergo nec in aeternitate Dei.

11. Item, nobilior est affirmatio quam negatio, et habitus quam privatio, et [59d] esse quam non-esse. Sed esse naturae non mensuratur aeternitate, ergo multo magis nec non-esse.

12. Item, simplicius est nunc aeternitatis quam nunc temporis infinitum. Ergo, si propter simplicitatem instantis temporalis non praecessit in eo esse nec non-esse creaturae, ergo multo magis in nunc aeternitatis non possunt stare simul esse et non-esse. Sed si non-esse creaturae fuit in aeternitate, et postea suum esse est in aeternitate, opposita sunt in ipsa aeternitate. Ergo hoc est impossibile, quod hic ponatur aliquod fundamentum, scilicet esse ex nihilo.

13. Item, si aliquid factum est ex nihilo, simul fuit ens et non-ens. Probatio: quod tantum natura praecedit alterum potest simul esse cum illo, sicut natura [sonus] praecedit cantum,[6] et tamen simul tempore generatur. Sed si creatura habuit aliquando non-esse, suum non-esse solum natura praecessit suum esse; ergo etc. Probatio assumptae: quia certum est quod non fuit prius tempore, nec prius aeternitate, quia tunc sequitur quod tempus esset post aeternitatem; quod falsum est, quia simul est cum ipsa.

14. Item, si creatura est et non fuit, si affirmatio et negatio de eodem, ergo idem suppositum est subtractum esse; et quod prius subtractum fuit puro[7] non-esse; et ita esse et purum non-esse aliquid habent commune, quod est falsum. Respondebatur quod idem est commune secundum rationem.

---

[6] [sonus] *lacuna in text*; supplied from St. Augustine, *Sonus cantum (praecedit origine)* in *Confession.* XII, c. 29, n. 40 (PL 32, 842; CSEL 33, 340).

[7] puro *corr. marg. for* po *in text.*

10. Further, if *non-esse* precedes *esse*, it does so by priority of nature or by temporal priority or by eternal priority. Not by priority of nature since nothingness implies neither nature nor an order of nature. Not by temporal priority, since time did not exist before *esse*. Not by eternal priority because the eternity of God is God Himself. But nothingness itself is not in God; nor is it, therefore, in God's eternity.

11. Again, affirmation is nobler than negation, habit nobler than privation, and *esse* nobler than *non-esse*. But the *esse* of nature is not measured by eternity; still less, therefore, is *non-esse*.

12. Further, the now of eternity is simpler than the now of time. If, therefore, because of the simplicity of the temporal instant, there is no precedence within it either of *esse* or of *non-esse* in the created order, then still less can *esse* and *non-esse* stand together simultaneously in the now of eternity. But, if the *non-esse* of a creature was in eternity, and then afterward its *esse* is in eternity, they are opposed within eternity itself. It is impossible, therefore, to put this down as something fundamental, namely, that *esse* comes from nothing.

13. Again, if something was made out of nothing, it was both being and non-being at the same time. Proof: what precedes another only in nature can exist simultaneously with that other. For example, sound precedes song by nature and is nonetheless generated simultaneously with it in time. But if at some time or other a creature had *non-esse*, its *non-esse* preceded its *esse* only in nature; therefore, etc. Proof of the assumption: it is certain that *non-esse* was not prior in time or in eternity because then it would follow that time came after eternity. And this is false because time is simultaneous with it.

14. Further, if the creature is and was not, and if there is both an affirmation and a negation about the same thing, then the subject of the propositions is the same minus *esse*. But that prior thing from which *esse* was removed was pure *non-esse*: and so *esse* and *pure non-esse* have something in common. But this is false. In reply it was said that the common element is only conceptual.

15. Contra: secundum rem vere et proprie quod est non fuit, et quod non fuit est; idem ergo est commune; ergo etc.

16. Item, omne quod fit, possibile erat fieri antequam fieret.[8] Si ergo aliquid est creatum de nihilo, prius potuit creari. Sed potentia non est sine possibili. Ergo quod creatur fuit aliquid antequam crearetur. Respondebatur quod non fuit nisi in potentia Creatoris.

17. Contra: "In aeternis non differt esse et posse,"[9] quia omnipotentia suo actui semper coniunctum est; ergo nullam habet actum ex temporis novitate.

18. Item, quia dicebatur quod posse creari non dicit potentiam nisi rationis, contra: posse creare et posse creari sunt diversorum subiectorum, quia posse creare est agentis primi, posse creari est ipsius creabilis. Ergo differunt essentialiter istae duae potentiae. Ergo, sicut vere differunt Creator et creatum, sic vere creare et posse creari.

19. Item, hoc probatur quia differunt, quia potentiae differunt sicut causae. Sed posse creare terminatur ad creationem actionem, posse creari ad creationem passionem. Ergo sicut creatio actio et creatio passio differunt essentialiter, sic istae potentiae. Ergo, si aliquid est creatum, praecessit potentia vera; quod repugnat creationi; ergo etc.

20. Item, creatio est actio. Actio autem requirit non quid agat, sed in quid agat. Ergo praesupponit materiam.

[8] Cf. St. Thomas, *Summa theol.* I, 45. 2, arg. 3 (248b 42–52).
[9] Aristotle, *Physic.* III, text 32, c. 4 (203b 29).

15. But to the contrary: the common element is truly and properly real; truly and properly what [now] is was not, and what was not [now] is. Consequently, there is a common element; therefore, etc.

16. Again, anything which comes to be could come to be before it came to be. If, therefore, something was created out of nothing, it was antecedently possible that such a thing be created. But there is no potency without a possible. What was created, therefore, was something before it was created. In reply it was said that it was something only in the potency of the Creator.

17. But to the contrary: "In eternal entities 'to be' and 'to be able' do not differ," since by omnipotence the "to be" and the "to be able" is each joined to its act; hence what is done gets nothing real from the newness of time.[1]

18. Further, since it is said that "to be able to be created" does not say potency except in the conceptual order, it is argued to the contrary that "to be able to create" and "to be able to be created" belong to different subjects, since "to be able to create" is a property of the First Cause, while "to be able to be created" is a property of what can be created. These two potencies, therefore, differ essentially. Hence, just as Creator and created truly differ, so too do "to create" and "to be able to be created."

19. Again, this is proved thus: they differ because the potencies differ just as the causes do. But "to be able to create" terminates in creation as *actio*, while "to be able to be created" terminates in creation as *passio*. Consequently, just as creation as *actio* differs essentially from creation as *passio*, so also do those potencies. If, therefore, something was created, a true potency preceded it; but this contradicts creation. Therefore, etc.

20. Further, creation is an *actio*. *Actio*, however, requires not something which acts but something on which it acts. Hence it presupposes matter.

---

[1] The Latin text here may be faulty.

21. Item, Deus est causa creaturae in triplici genere causae: efficientis, formalis et finalis. Ad agendum non indiget alio efficiente, quia ipse est virtus infinita et est ipse sua virtus, nec agit alio[10] a se. Item, nec indiget alio exemplari a se diverso ad producendum, quia ipse [est] essentialiter exemplar. Nec eget alio fine, quia ipse est finis ultimus. Sed si exemplar differret ab esse essentialiter, indigeret alio exemplari a se diverso ad producendum. Similiter de virtute et fine. Ergo cum materia, quae est quarta causa, ab eo sit penitus diversa, non potest agere nisi praesupposita materia.

22. Item, si educitur de non-esse in esse: aut quando est, aut quando non est. Si educitur quando est: sed quod est non eget eductione,[11] et quod non eget, non educitur. Ergo non creatur quando est.

23. Item, si creatura accipit esse vel si fit de non-creante creans, hoc est per mutationem ipsius creantis. Probatio: quia non est per mutationem creaturae, quia Deus creat antequam creatura creetur; creatio enim eius [= est] actio aeterna. — Respondetur quod creatio connotat effectum. — Contra: nihil connotat nisi quod dicitur de creante; connotat ergo [60a] actionem et non passionem. Actio autem non est sine termino actionis. Ergo prius est creatura quam actio. — Item, duplex est creatio: creatio actio et creatio passio. Sed creatio passio est accidens creati. Sed nullum accidens est prius suo subiecto. Ergo impossibile est creationem passionem praecedere creatum. Sed creatum non posset esse nisi praecederet illud ordine naturae creatio passio, cum sit via ad esse. Via autem praecedit terminum; ergo etc.

---

[10] alio] alio id est per aliud *add. marg.* **F**[2].
[11] eductione] vel eductore *add. marg.* **F**[2].

21. Again, God is the cause of a creature by three kinds of causality: efficient, formal, and final. In order to act God does not need another efficient cause because He is infinite power, and He Himself is His own power. And He does not act by means of anything other than Himself. Further, God does not need any other model [exemplar] distinct from Himself in order to produce anything, because He Himself is essentially the model [exemplar]. Nor does He need another final cause, since He Himself is the ultimate end.[2] But if the model [exemplar] were to differ essentially from being, it would need another model [exemplar] distinct from itself in order to produce anything. The same is true of efficient and final causality. Since, therefore, matter, the fourth cause, is totally different from God, God cannot act unless matter is presupposed.

22. Further, suppose something is educed from *non-esse* into *esse*. This happens either when that something is or when it is not. If it is educed when it is, then what already is does not need to be educed. What does need to be deduced, is not educed. Consequently, when something [already] is, it is not created.

23. Again, if a creature receives *esse*, or if something becomes a creator from being a non-creator, this comes about through a change in the creating agency itself. Proof: it does not come about through a change in the creature since God creates before the creature is created. For creation is God's eternal *actio*. In reply it is said that creation connotes its effect. But to the contrary: creation connotes nothing except what is said of the creating agent. It connotes *actio*, therefore, and not *passio*. But there is no *actio* without a terminus. The creature, therefore, is prior to *actio*. Furthermore, creation is twofold: creation as *actio* and creation as *passio*. But creation as *passio* is an accident in what is created. But no accident is prior to its subject. It is impossible, therefore, for creation as *passio* to precede what is created. But what is created could not exist unless creation as *passio* preceded it in the order of nature, since the latter is the road to the former. A road, however, comes before the destination; therefore, etc.

[2] This sentence seems to be misplaced in the manuscript or else it is just superfluous.

24. Item, potentia creabilis remotior est ab actu quam potentia numeri, quia potentia creabilis nihil dicit in actu aut potentia reali. Potentia autem numeralis dicit aliquid in actu in quo fundatur realis potentia. Sed potentia numeri ad infinitas species non potest educi in actu; ergo multo magis nec potentia creabilis.

25. Item, materia nullo modo potest esse a Primo. Hoc probatur, quia omne agens agit secundum quod est in actu.

26. Item, agens a proposito educit sibi simile in specie. Sed materia est ens penitus[12] in potentia. Deus autem est ens plene in actu. Ergo non habet aliquam convenientiam materia cum Deo; ergo ab ipso esse non potest.

27. Item, in creaturis sunt multi defectus. Aut igitur sunt in creaturis unde ex nihilo, aut ratione materiae. Si primo modo, tunc omnes creaturae aeque plenae sunt defectibus; quod falsum est. Si ratione materiae, ergo materia non est a Deo ex nihilo; vel si ipsa est ex nihilo, adhuc omnia erunt aeque plena defectibus[13] quaecumque ipsam participant.

28. Item, si aliquid creatur, aut materia [est] aut forma aut compositum. Si est compositum, contra: actio indivisibilis non terminatur ad divisibile. Sed creatio est actio indivisibilis; ergo non terminatur ad compositum. Quod est indivisibilis patet, quia est summae simplicitatis et in [ens] indivisibiliter terminatur, quia nihil est medium inter ens et non-ens. Item, nec materia creatur, quia actio nobilissima non terminatur ad summum ignobile. Materia autem est summe ignobilis. Item, nec materia [= forma] creatur, nec [= quia] forma praesupponit materiam; ergo etc.

---

[12] penitus] est ens *repeated*; I have placed the words after *autem*, where they evidently belong.
[13] A cross in margin would indicate the text is incomplete.

24. Further, the capacity for being created is further removed from act than the capacity for number. The reason is that capacity for being created says nothing either in act or in real potency. The capacity for number, however, says something in act in which a real potency is grounded. But number's capacity for infinity cannot actually be educed; still less, therefore, can the capacity for being created.

25. Again, matter can in no way be by the agency of the First Being. Proof: every agent acts according to what is in act.

26. Further, an agent which deliberates educes something similar in kind to itself. But matter is being completely in potency. God, however, is being fully in act. Matter, therefore, has no affinity with God. It cannot, therefore, be through His agency.

27. Again, there are many defects in creatures. These defects, therefore, are in creatures either because they come from nothing or because of matter. If the first, then all creatures are equally full of defects; but this is false. If because of matter, then matter is not made by God out of nothing. Or if it is made out of nothing, then all things whatsoever which share in matter will be equally full of defects.

28. Further, if anything is created, it is either matter or form or a composite. Suppose it is a composite; then to the contrary it may be argued that an indivisible *actio* does not terminate in something divisible. But creation is an indivisible *actio*; consequently, it does not terminate in something composite. It is evident that creation is indivisible because it has the greatest simplicity and terminates indivisibly in being, since there is no middle ground between being and non-being. Further, matter is not created, because the noblest *actio* does not terminate in the most ignoble thing. But matter is the most ignoble thing. Again, matter is not created, and form does not presuppose matter; therefore, etc.

CONTRA:

a. Avicenna, VI *Meta*.:[14] "Philosophi non intelligunt per agentem principium mutationis [= motionis] tantum, sicut intelligunt naturales, sed principium essendi et creatorem [= datorum] eius, sicut est creator mundi."

b. Item, causa quanto prior, tanto prius [= plus] influit.[15] Ergo prima influit super totum.

c. Item, materia est secundum quam unumquodque potest esse et non esse, secundum Philosophum.[16] Ergo materia multum communicat cum non-esse. Si ergo forma est productibilis, quae dat esse, multo magis materia est productibilis, a qua est non-esse. Sed materia non producitur de materia, quia sic esset ire in infinitum; ergo producitur de nihilo.

d. Item, agens quod agit secundum aliquid sui, per virtutem suam scilicet, potest reproducere secundum partem, ut fit per generationem in qua transit commune subiectum a specie in speciem. Ergo agens quod agit secundum se totum, cuius [= cui?] subest sua actio, producit rem secundum suam totam essentiam, scilicet secundum materiam et formam.[17]

e. Item, duplex est actio Dei, intrinseca et extrinseca. Ergo, sicut intrinseca productio ostendit infinitatem Dei, sic et extrinseca debet[18] manifestare infinitam potentiam Dei. Sed hoc non est nisi . . .

---

[14] VI Meta.] dicenti *ms*. Cf. Avicenna, *Metaph*. VI, c. 1 (ed. Venice 1508, 91b).

[15] Cf. St. Bonaventure, *In II Sent*., d. 1. p. 1, a. 1, q. 1, fund. 1; *Opera omnia* II (ed. Quaracchi 1885), 14b; whence we have interpreted *prius* as plus. The argument depends on the *Liber de causis* prop. 1; ed. A. Pattin (Louvain s.a.), 46.

[16] Aristotle, *Metaph*. VI (VII), c. 1 (1042a 25–28).

[17] Cf. St. Bonaventure, loc. cit., 14b–15a.

[18] debet] decet (docet?) F. The final word (*nisi*) is followed by a lacuna of some three lines.

To The Contrary:

a. Avicenna, VI *Metaphysics*, says: "By 'agent' the philosophers [metaphysicians] do not understand the principle of change alone as the naturalists [scientists] do, but also the principle of being and its creator, just as there is a creator of the world."

b. Again the scope of a cause's influence is in proportion to its priority. The first cause, therefore, has influence upon the whole.

c. Further, matter is that by which each thing can be or not be, as the Philosopher says. Matter, therefore, has much in common with *non-esse*. If, therefore, form can be made and if form gives *esse*, still more matter can be made as the principle of *non-esse*. But matter is not made out of matter, since this would lead to an infinite regress; consequently it is made out of nothing.

d. Again, an agent that acts according to something proper to it, i.e., by its own power, can reproduce a thing in part. This happens, for example, through generation in which a common subject goes from one species to another. Consequently, an agent that acts according to its entire self, i.e., whose *actio* is entirely under its control, produces a thing according to its entire essence, that is according to matter and form.

e. Again, the *actio* of God is twofold, intrinsic and extrinsic. Consequently, just as intrinsic production shows forth God's infinity, so too extrinsic production ought to manifest God's infinite potency. But this is not the case unless . . .

RESPONSIO:

I. Creatio est articulus fidei et nunquam ad plenum alicui infideli illuxit.[19] Hinc et quod quidam posuerunt mundum omnino a Deo non fuisse productum, sicut recitat Augustinus, *De civitate* XI, cap. 4, dicens contra eos: "Mobilitas et immobilitas partium mundanarum ad idem tendentium clamat totum mundum habere idem principium." Alii peius [60b] errantes, quia non potuerunt intelligere aliquid fieri ex nihilo, mundum istum factum esse de Dei substantia posuerunt. Quod etiam per eandem viam improbatur. In pluribus enim locis probat Augustinus[20] animam non fuisse factam esse de Dei substantia ideo quod mutabilis est. Et ideo alii, ut Platonici, [posuerunt][21] mundum esse productum [ex materia] praeexistenti aeterna et increata. Unde Ambrosius, in *Hexaëmeron*:[22] "Plato tria posuit increata et sine initio: Deum et exemplar et materiam. Deum vero non tanquam creatorem materiae, sed tanquam artificem." Propter quod Philosophus dicit:[23] "Plato solus generat mundum."

---

[19] Cf. St. Bonaventure, *In II Sent.*, d. 1, p. 1, a. 1, q. 1, resp. (II, 16b); and St. Thomas, *Summa theol.* I, 46, 2, resp. (297a11 ff.). — What follows from Augustine is rather a paraphrase of *De civitate Dei* XI, c. 4, n. 2: "Exceptis enim propheticis vocibus, mundus ipse ordinatissima sua mutabilitate et mobilitate et visibilium omnium pulcherrima specie quodammodo tacitus et factum se esse, et nonnisi a Deo . . . fieri se potuisse proclamat" (PL 41, 319; CSEL, 40–1, 515; CCL 48, 324).

[20] Cf. *De Genesi ad litt.*, VII, c. 2, n. 3, and c. 3, n. 5 (PL 42, 356, 357; CSEL 28–1, 202, 203); and especially *Contra adversarium legis et prophetarum* I, c. 14, nn. 21–22 (PL 42, 614f.); and Peter Lombard, *Sent.* II, d. 17, c. 1, n. 5 (Quaracchi 1970) I, 410f.

[21] The text is marked by a cross in the margin; I have essayed to repair it.

[22] Book I, c. 1 (PL 14 [1845], 123A; CSEL 32, 3); cf. P. Lombard, *Sent.* II, d. 1, c. 1, n. 2 (ed. cit. 330), where Strabus is quoted to the same effect.

[23] Cf. *Physic.* VIII, c. 1 (251b 17–18). More exactly, as used by other scholastics, the authority should perhaps read: *Solus Plato genuit tempus*; cf. Gérard of Abbeville, *Quodl.* XIV, q. 10; ed. Ph. Grand, "Le Quodlibet XIV de Gérard d'Abbeville: La vie de Gérard d'Abbeville," *Archives d'hist. doctr. et litt. du moyen âge* 31 (1964) 267.

SOLUTION:

I. Creation is an article of faith and never became completely clear to any infidel. And so, some posited a world not produced at all by God, as Augustine says in *De civitate* XI, ch. 4, arguing against them: "The fact that the parts of the world, whether in motion or at rest, tend to one and the same thing proclaims that the entire world has one and the same source." Others made still worse mistakes in that they held this world to have been made out of God's own substance, since they could not understand that something is made out of nothing. This position, too, is rejected in the same way. For in many places Augustine proves that the soul was not made from God's substance because it is subject to change. And so others, like the Platonists, held that the world was made out of pre-existing, eternal, and uncreated matter. Wherefore, Ambrose in the *Hexaëmeron* says: "Plato held that there are three realities which are uncreated and without beginning: God, model [exemplar], and matter. God indeed is not the Creator of matter but its craftsman." For this reason the Philosopher says, "Plato alone generates the world."

Sed istud primo improbatur, quia unumquodque quanto durabilius est tanto melius est. Si igitur materia omnibus aliis durabilior est, omnibus aliis melior est. — Item, quantitas rei cognoscitur per virtutis mensuram et materialis [?]. Ergo, si materia habet mensuram infinitam, habet et virtutem infinitam, quod est impossibile. — Item, Richardus probat, *De Trinitate* V,[24] quod eo ipso quod persona Patris non est ad aliam, omnis alia persona et natura est ab ipsa. Et probat sic: quoniam si habet esse a se, non habet esse [secundum] participationem essendi; et si non secundum participationem, ergo secundum plenitudinem. Sed ubi est plenitudo essentiae et potentiae, ibi est omnino posse, quia suum posse est omne posse. Ergo ex ipsa est omne posse et omne esse. — Item, negare non potest quin esse a se sit nobilissima conditio et proprietas principii. Ergo si materia est a se, convenit in nobilissima proprietate cum primo principio.

Item, si materia est increata: aut simplex est aut composita. Si simplex est, penitus ergo de ipsa nunquam fiet compositum, nisi pars compositi fiat de nihilo. Si autem sit composita, omnis compositio est a componente simplici. Ergo necesse est aliam esse causam materiae, et ita non est a se. — Item, esse a se dicit proprietatem dignitatis et actum nobilem essendi, ut dictum est.[25] Ergo convenit rei digniori. Sed dignior est forma quam materia. Ergo si non convenit formae, nec convenit materiae. — Item, quod est alterius causa amittendi esse, ipsum esse non habet ex se. Sed contrariorum contrariae sunt causae. Sed materia est in quolibet quod potest non esse; ergo etc.

De rerum vero principio primo non habet Aristoteles manifestam sententiam, quamvis dicat quod non est virtus nisi a Deo.[26]

[24] Ch. 4 (PL 196, 951 D; ed. J. Ribaillier [Paris 1958] 199). Cf. John Pecham, *In I Sent.*, d. 27, q. 1, a. 1: "Igitur primitas Patris innascibilitate significatur; et quia eo ipso quo innascibilis est, a nullo est, sequitur ut omne aliud et omnis alia res quaecumque sit ab ipso, sicut docet Richardus *De trin.* 5 c. 4 . . . Ergo innascibilitas Patrem distinguit aliquo modo, immo ut supra habetur ex Richardo, rationem dicit communicandi"; cod. Florent. Bibl. Naz. *Conv. soppr.* G. 4, *854*, f. 80d; cited by M. Schmaus, *Der Liber propugnatorius des Thomas Anglicus und die Lehrunterschiede zwischen Thomas von Aquin und Duns Scotus*, BGPTMA 29 (Münster 1930) 586, note 57.
[25] Cf. some seven lines above.
[26] Cf. *Ethic. Nic.* I, c. 9 (1099b 10), and II, c. 1 (1103a 25).

But in the first place this position is rejected because the more lasting something is, the better it is. If, therefore, matter is more lasting than everything else, then it is better than everything else. Further, the quantity of a thing is known by measuring its power, even material power[?].³ Consequently, if matter has an infinite measure, it also has infinite power. But this is impossible. Again, in *De Trinitate* V Richard proves that precisely because the Person of the Father is not in relation to something prior, every other person and nature is from Him. His proof is this: if the Father had *esse* from Himself, He does not have it by participation in being; and if He does not have it by participation, then He has it by fullness. But where there is fullness of essence and potency, there is total capacity to act, since His capacity is every capacity. Hence every capacity and every *esse* is from Him. Again, it cannot be denied that *esse a se* is the noblest condition and property of any principle. If, therefore, matter is *a se*, it shares with the first principle the noblest property.

Further, suppose matter is uncreated. Then it is either simple or composite. If it is simple, then in no way at all will a composite be made out of it, unless a part of the composite be made out of nothing. If it is composite, however, then every composition is made up of simple components. There must, therefore, be another cause of matter, and so matter is not *a se*. Again, *esse a se* says a property of dignity and a noble act of being, as we have said. Hence it belongs to a more worthy reality. But form is more worthy than matter. Consequently, if it does not belong to form, it does not belong to matter either. Again, what is the cause of another's losing *esse* does not have *esse* of itself. But the causes of contraries are contraries. But matter is in whatever can cease to be; therefore, etc.

Concerning the true first principle of things Aristotle does not have any clear-cut opinion, although he says there is no power except from God.

---

³ There seems to be something wrong with the Latin text here.

II. Hi igitur errores omnes professione fidei excluduntur, dicente Scriptura quia *In principio creavit Deus caelum et terram*.[27] Hanc veritatem fidei nullus sapientum mundi intellexit ad plenum, quia aut eam negaverunt aut erronee posuerunt, sicut Avicenna, qui sic eam attribuit Creatori quod etiam eam attribuit creaturae.[28] Et idcirco omnibus his erroribus praeexclusis, sciendum est omnia in primo instanti temporis fuisse producta de nihilo.

Ad cuius intelligentiam sequestranda est imaginatio philosophorum naturalium qui quaerunt commune subiectum, et ad intellectualem indaginem, ut est possibile, ascendendum. Quod igitur omnia sint ex nihilo creata, patet tam considerando conditiones ipsius Creatoris quam etiam ipsius creaturae.

Primo, dico, attendamus quantitatem potentiae [a parte producentis][29] quoniam quanto potentia est virtuosior, tanto paucioribus indiget adminiculis et dispositioni ad productionem sui effectus.[30] Ergo potentia quae [in]finite excedit omnem alteram potentiam circa aliquid producendum, infinite minus requirit quam alia potentia. Sed infinite minus quocumque ente non est nisi pure non-ens. Ergo infinita potentia eo quo infinita potest producere quemcumque effectum de pure non-ente. Unde Hugo I *De sacramentis*, parte 1, cap. 1:[31] "Omnipotentiae virtus ineffabilis, sicut non poterat aliud praeter se habere coaeternum quo in faciendo iuvaretur, ita sibi cum voluit suberat ut quod voluit et quando et quantum [60c] voluit de nihilo crearetur."

---

[27] Gen. 1, 1.

[28] *Metaph.* IX, c. 4 (f. 104d–105a); cf. St. Thomas, *Summa theologiae* I, 45, 5, resp. (288a 35ff.).

[29] The manuscript has a lacuna of some ten letters; since the argument follows St. Bonaventure, we have supplied the omission from *In I Sent.*, d. 1, p. 1, a. 1, q. 1, fund. 2 (II, 14b).

[30] Cf. Aristotle, *De caelo* II, t. 62, c. 12 (292b 4ss); the argument is taken from St. Bonaventure, loc. cit.

[31] PL 176, 187 B; quoted by St. Thomas, *De aet. mundi*, n. 10.

II. All these errors, therefore, are excluded by the profession of faith, as Scripture says, "In the beginning God created heaven and earth." None of the wise of the world completely understood this truth of faith because either they denied it, or held it in an erroneous way, as Avicenna did, who attributed it to Creator and creature alike. And so when all these errors are removed, it should be seen that all things were made out of nothing in the first instant of time.

To understand this we must go beyond the imagination of natural philosophers who seek a common subject, and we must ascend as far as possible to an intellectual capture of the topic. That everything was created out of nothing is evident, therefore, from a consideration of the conditions both of the Creator and of the creature.

First, I say, let us consider the amount of potency on the part of the Maker, since to the extent that the potency is more powerful, fewer helps are needed to dispose it to produce its effect. Hence a potency which infinitely surpasses every other potency with respect to producing something requires infinitely less than any other potency. But to be infinitely less than any being is to be nothing but pure non-being. Infinite potency, therefore, insofar as it is infinite, can produce any effect out of pure non-being. So Hugo I in *De sacramentis*, part I, ch. 1, says: "Just as the ineffable power of omnipotence could not have anything coeternal with itself by which it was aided in producing something, so too, when it willed, it had in its power to create from nothing what and when and how much it willed."

Secundo, hoc idem patet considerando modum producendi res in esse. Agit enim per intellectum suum, per Verbum suum, quod est ipsa eius operativa potentia, nec differunt in eo cognitio et operativa potentia, sicut in omni creatura differunt. Sicut igitur eadem facilitate intellectus divinus apprehendit entia et non-entia, sic necesse est ut virtus eius eadem facilitate producere possit aliquid sicut de ente, ita de non-ente. Unde Augustinus, *Confessionum* XI:[32] "Verbo tibi coaeterno et sempiterno dicis omnia quae dicis, et sic quidquid dicis ut fiat non aliter quam illo facis."

Item, idem patet tertio considerando perfectionem divini exemplaris, quia perfectiones divinae sunt exemplaria creaturarum exprimendo se in creatura. Sicut igitur omne vivens est a Deo sub ratione vitae, immo vita eius est exemplar omnis vitae, ita esse in eo est exemplar omnis esse. — Item, quia esse divinum est omnipotentius[33] in exprimendo quam vivere divinum, immo quodammodo perfectius in causando in quantum generalius se diffundit, quod tamen ut in Deo est nullum dicit gradum, unde Dionysius, V *De divinis nominibus*:[34] "Nihil est exsistens cuius non sit substantia et aevum ipsum esse. Convenientius igitur cunctis aliis principalius." Ergo non habet minus de vi expressiva quam aliae perfectiones divinae, "sicut exsistens Deus laudatur ex digniore donorum aliorum eius." Igitur, cum Deus sit esse purum et perfectum, necesse est ut illud suum esse sit expressivum cuiuslibet alterius esse, ut sicut unum [= una] vita dat vivere non-viventi, sic unum ens dat esse simpliciter non-enti. Unde in eodem capitulo:[35] "Ante alias ipsius participationes esse propositum est, et est[36] ipsum, secundum se esse senius eo quod est per se vitae esse," etc.

Et haec est sententia Avicennae in loco auctoritatis allegatae.[37] Item, dicit alibi, eodem libro, quod "creatio est dignior omnibus modis dandi esse."

---

[32] Chapt. 7 (PL 32, 813; CSEL 33, 287).
[33] est omnipotentius] enim est impotentius F.
[34] Num. 5 (PG 3, 820 B; *Dionysiaca* I, ed. Chevalier [Solesmii 1937], 338).
[35] Num. 5 (PG 3, 820 A; *Dionysiaca* I, 337).
[36] est] quoniam *add.* F. Then below, for *senius*, the codex reads *se minus* (with cross over it).
[37] Cf. note 28 above; then *Metaph.* VI, c. 2 (f. 92a).

Second, the same is evident from a consideration of the way in which a thing is brought into existence. For God acts through His intellect, through His Word, which itself is His capacity to produce effects. In Him cognition and capacity to produce effects do not differ as they do in all creatures. Consequently, just as the divine intellect apprehends with equal facility beings and non-beings, so too it must be that His power can produce with equal facility something out of nothing and something out of being. So Augustine says in *Confessions*, IX: "All that You say You say by the Word, everlasting and coeternal with Yourself, and so whatever You say is to be, You make in no other way than by saying it."

Further, in the third place, the same is evident from a consideration of the perfection of the divine model [exemplar], since the divine perfections are the models [exemplars] of creatures by which God expresses Himself in the creature. Hence just as every living thing is from God under the title of life (indeed God's life is the exemplar of all life), so *esse* in Him is the exemplar of every *esse*. Again, since the divine *esse* is more omnipotent than the divine life in expressing itself, it is indeed in some way more perfect as a cause insofar as it pours itself out more universally. And this is true even though in God there is nothing which says degree. So says Dionysius in *De divinis nominibus* V: "Nothing exists whose substance and eternity is not *Esse* itself. And rightly so because *esse* is more basic than all the others." *Esse* does not have less expressive force, therefore, than the other divine perfections, "just as God, as existing, is praised for the more worthy of His other gifts." Consequently, since God is pure and perfect *esse*, it must be that His own *esse* be expressive of every other *esse*, so that, just as one life gives life to the non-living, so one being gives *esse* to what is simply non-being. In the same chapter he says: "Before other participations in Him there is *esse*, and *esse* in itself is prior to life itself," etc.

And this is Avicenna's opinion cited above. In another place in the same book he says, "creation is a worthier way of giving *esse* than all others."

1. Ad obiectum primum dicendum quod Deus potest quidquid in se est possibile et suae perfectioni non repugnat. Tunc autem illud in quo contradictio implicatur cadit a ratione, sicut ubi est contradictionis implicatio; verbi gratia in omni impossibili per accidens. Tanta enim est impossibilitas ut pransus fieret ieiunus, sicut ut corruptus fieret incorruptus. Quia igitur corruptio transit in praeteritum, non potest non fuisse facta, et ita corruptam fieri virginem implicat contradictionem.[38]

2. Ad secundum dicendum quod non est simile, quia esse creaturae non excludit non fuisse, sicut esse virginem excludit esse corruptam.

3. Ad tertium dicendum quod abusiva est comparatio cum dicitur quod "maior est" etc., quia in comparando creaturam Deo sunt deo extrema: in comparando creaturam nihilo, non est nisi unum extremum, quorum unum caret omni possibilitate pro utroque extremo mutationis. Non sic creatura, quia in nihilo non est possibilitas, sed tantum esse creaturae est possibile.

4. Ad quartum dicendum quod revera non est ibi distantia, quia non est nisi unum extremum; et ideo proprie non pertransitur, quia extrema non concurrunt vel sequuntur se circa idem supremum.

5. Ad quintum dicendum, sicut patet, quod ibi non est distantia. Item, extremum distantiae inter Creatorem et creaturam caret omni possibilitate initiali et finali.

6. Ad sextum dicendum quod hoc est in hac productione singulare, quia contactus est causa huius quod tangitur in tactu suo. Unde, quia ipse tactus dat esse, prius natura est tactus quam sit res ipsa quae tangitur. — Ad obiectum autem quod dicit quod tangi est esse tactum et esse tactum addit supra esse,

---

[38] Cf. St. Thomas, *Summa theologiae* I, 25, 4, resp. (175a 48–175b 18); and *Quodl.* V., q. 2, a. 1.

1. Reply to the first objection: God can do whatever is possible in itself and whatever does not contradict its own perfection. But then that in which a contradiction is implied becomes just as unreasonable, as the implication of a contradiction itself: for example, in every case where something is impossible *per accidens*. This sort of impossibility is as great in the case of a well-fed person's becoming a starving person, as in the case of a corrupted person becoming uncorrupted. Since, then, the corruption passes into history, it cannot not have happened, and thus that a corrupted woman become a virgin implies a contradiction.

2. Reply to the second objection: we deny the similarity, since the "to be" of a creature does not exclude "not to have been" in the same way that "to be a virgin" excludes "to have been corrupted."

3. Reply to the third objection: where it says, "There is a greater . . . "the comparison is bad, since in comparing God and creature there are two termini, while in comparing the creature to nothingness there is but one, and that one terminus lacks all possibility of being either terminus in the process of change. This is not the case with a creature, because in nothingness there is no possibility while the *esse* of a creature is possible.

4. Reply to the fourth objection: there really is no distance there at all, since there is only one extreme. And so, properly speaking, there is no "traversing," because termini neither concur nor follow after one another relative to the same supreme infinite.

5. Reply to the fifth objection: it is evident that there is no distance there either. Further, any terminus in distance between Creator and creature could not be either a beginning or an end point.

6. Reply to the sixth objection: this is peculiar to that sort of production, since contact is the cause of what is touched in its very act of touching. Whence it follows that, since the touching itself gives *esse*, the touching is by nature prior to the thing as touched.—Still, to the objection which says that "to be

ergo posterius est eo, respondeo quod illud addit super alterum secundum rem vel sicut tactum ab ipso vel [sicut] cursu rerum naturali posterius est eo quia addit super eum secundum rem. Sed in proposito addit secundum modum loquendi, quia quod additur non causatur a principiis subiecti nec ordine, nec sequitur ipsum, sed naturaliter praecedit sicut creari.

7. Ad septimum breviter respondeo quod omnes negativae concedendae sunt in talibus et nulla affirmativa. Haec enim vera est [60d]: creatura non fuit nisi in instanti [A]. Haec autem falsa: prius fuit suum non-esse, quia per hoc ponitur mensura distincta a tempore secundum prius et posterius; et propter hoc non est dandum aliquod instans prius per modum aeternitatis, sicut nec extra mundum datus est locus, videlicet ubi est. Tamen divina maiestas transcendit mundi capacitatem. Sicut qui de [= quidem?] aeternitatis [sempiternitas?],[39] sic est prius quod est simul cum tempore et semper. Unde inter nunc temporis primum et aeternitatem quae semper fuit, nihil cadit medium. — Concedo ergo quod mundus incepit et non fuit prius. Et nego istam: suum non-esse fuit prius quam suum [esse], quia hoc ponit mensuram distinctam a tempore secundum prius et posterius. Unde concedi potest ista: mundus semper fuit. Unde Augustinus, *De civitate* XII, cap. 15:[40] "Angeli, si semper fuerunt, creati sunt; ac per hoc nec si semper fuerunt ideo Creatori coaeterni sunt. Ille enim semper fuit aeternitate incommutabili, isti autem facti sunt: sed ideo semper fuisse dicuntur, quia omni tempore fuere."

---

[39] A conjectural reading to fill in a lacuna of 8 letters.
[40] Num. 2 (or in modern edd., c. 16); the original text is somewhat varied (PL 41, 364; CSEL 40-1, 593; CCL 48, 372).

touched" (*tangi*) is "to be" (*esse*) plus "touched" (*tactum*) and so "to be touched" adds something to "to be," and thus comes after "to be," I reply that "touched" adds something to "to be" in the real order in the same way as "touched" (either by a personal agent or in the natural course of events) comes after "to be" in the real order, that is, in that it adds something [touched] to it [to be]. But in the proposition under consideration [creation], it "created" adds something [to the "to be" of what is created] only in a manner of speaking, since what is added is caused neither by the subject's own nature nor by the order of nature; nor does it follow *esse* but rather precedes it naturally, just as "to be" precedes "to be created."

7. Reply to the seventh objection: briefly, in such matters all the negative statements are to be conceded, but none of the affirmative. For this is true: the creature did not exist except in some instant (A). But this is false: the creature's *non-esse* existed before, since this posits a measure of before and after which is distinct from time. One ought not to concede, therefore, some prior instant in eternity, just as one did not concede that there is "place" outside the world, that is, a place where it [the world] is. Still, the divine majesty transcends the world's capacity. Just as, indeed, the everlastingness of eternity [is prior?], so too is that prior which is simultaneous with time and forever.[4] Consequently, between the first instant of time and eternity, which always was, there is no middle ground. I concede, therefore, that the world began and was not prior to its *esse*. And I deny that its *non-esse* was prior to its *esse*, since this posits a measure of before and after distinct from time. Whence this statement can be admitted: the world always was. So Augustine in *De civitate* XII, ch. 15, says: "Angels were created even though they always were; hence even if they always were, still they are not coeternal with the Creator. For the Creator always was in an unchangeable eternity, while these were made; but then they are said always to have been, because they were throughout all time."

---

[4] This line in the text is very corrupted.

9. Ad nonum dicendum quod sicut [Deus] non est extra mundum, ut "extra" dicat dimensionem positionis, cum non sit extra mundum per immensitatem virtutis quia continet mundum et mundo non collimitatur, ita fuit ante mundum, non quidem secundum extensionem sed secundum simplicem aeternitatem. Unde etiam [= dicit?] Augustinus, *De civitate* XII, cap. 15:[41] "Si Deus fuit semper dominus, semper habuit creaturam suo dominatui servientem, de nihilo factam nec sibi coaeternam; erat quippe ante illam quamvis nullo tempore sine illa; non eam spatio praecurrens, sed manente perpetuitate praecedens." Haec Augustinus. Igitur praecessit sine dimensionis extensione sicut transcendit mundum cui non collimitatur sine dimensione. — Item, Augustinus, *De civitate* XI, cap. 5: "Si dicunt inanes esse cogitationes quibus [infinita] imaginantur loca, cum nullus sit locus praeter mundum, respondetur eis isto modo inaniter cogitare homines praeterita tempora vacationis Dei, cum tempus nullum sit ante mundum."

10. Ad decimum dico quod non-esse non praecessit esse. Concedo enim negativas nihil ponentes, et nego omnes affirmativas ponentes durationem extensionis vel ordinatae secundum prioritatem respectu instantis temporis.

11. Ad undecimum dico quod verum concludit, quia nonesse omni mensura caret.

12. Ad duodecimum respondeo: Haec est falsa: "non-esse mundi fuit in nunc aeternitatis," quia puro non-esse nulla est mensura. Esse autem creaturae est in tempore. — Quod si adhuc velles omnino dicere quod non-esse fuisset in nunc aeternitatis, non est [idem] simplicitati instantis, quia simplicitas instantis est simplicitatis paucitatis vel arctationis, et ideo plura complecti non potest. Simplicitas autem nunc aeternitatis non est paucitatis sed multiplicitatis immensae, unde omnia tempora complectitur. — Quidem aliter dicunt quod non sequitur, quia non-esse mensuratur immediate ab aeternitate, esse autem mediate. Sed illic nihil est quia nobilius esset nonesse quam esse, quia immediatius aeternitati.

---

[41] Num. 3 or c. 16 (PL 41, 365; CSEL 40–1, 594; CCL 48, 372). — This is followed by a reference to Book XI, c. 5 (PL 41, 321; CSEL 40–1, 518, CCL 18, 326).

9. Reply to the ninth objection: one must say that just as God is not "outside" the world where "outside" says a dimension of position, although He is not outside the world through the immensity of His power since He contains the world and is not limited along with it, so too God was before the world not in terms of any spatial consideration, but in terms of His simple eternity. Thus Augustine too in *De civitate* XII, ch. 15, says: "If God always was Lord, the creature, made from nothing and not coeternal with Him, always was under His dominion; indeed He was before the creature even though at no time was He without it; God does not run before the creature in space, but goes before it by His enduring perpetuity." These are Augustine's words. God, therefore, preceded creatures without the extension implied in dimension, just as, without stretching, He transcends the world to which He is not limited. Again, Augustine in *De civitate* XI, ch. 5, says: "If they say that thoughts which imagine infinite places are empty, since outside the world there is no 'place,' they are answered thus: in vain do men think of past times when God had nothing to do, since before the world there is no time."

10. Reply to the tenth objection: I say that *non-esse* did not precede *esse*. For I concede the negative propositions which posit nothing, but I deny all affirmative propositions which posit a duration of extension, even one ordered by priority with respect to an instant of time.

11. Reply to the eleventh objection: its conclusion is true since *non-esse* lacks all measure.

12. Reply to the twelfth objection: the following is false: "the *non-esse* of the world was in the now of eternity." The reason is that what is pure *non-esse* has no measure. The *esse* of a creature, however, is in time. But if one still would wish to say that *non-esse* was in the now of eternity, then the now of eternity does not have the same simplicity as the instant of want and constraint and so it cannot embrace many things. The simplicity of the now of eternity, however, is not that of want but of immense multiplicity so that it includes all times. Others say that this does not follow since *non-esse* is measured immediately by eternity while *esse* only mediately. But there is nothing in it since then *non-esse* would be nobler than *esse* inasmuch as it would be closer to eternity.

13. Ad decimum tertium dico quod quomodocumque dicatur 'prius,' ista est falsa: 'prius fuit non-esse mundi quam esse mundi.' Haec autem vera: 'non prius fuit esse mundi,' quia, ut prius tactum est, dicendo 'prius fuit non-esse mundi' copulatur mensura habens prius et posterius respectu temporis ex necessario, quia omnis mensura habens prius respectu temporis aliquid habet se posterius, quia hic est sermo de prioritate extensionis.

14–15. Ad decimum quartum dicendum quod affirmatio et negatio est de eodem, non ut ente sed ut apprehenso ab intellectu. Res enim ut apprehenditur ab intellectu, apprehenditur absque suo esse vel suo non-esse. Non enim est suum esse. Aliquid ergo est commune utrique, non secundum rem, sed quantum ad intellectum; vel si secundum rationem, non tamen ut entem sed ut intellectu apprehensibilem. — Et sic patet ad decimum quintum.

16. Ad decimum sextum dicendum quod cum dicit 'omne quod fit, possibile erat fieri,' distinguo: quia si sit secundum cursum naturalem possibile est fieri secundum cursum naturalem; si vero sit supra cursum naturalem, possibile erat potentia supernaturali, potentia scilicet Creatoris, quae quantum ad intrinseca semper est actui coniuncta, quantum ad extrinseca minime.

17. Ad decimum septimum iam patet, quia de actu interiori verum est, de actu exteriori falsum est.

18. Ad decimum octavum dicendum quod possibile circa aliquid dicitur proprie secundum potentiam quae est in ipso. Large tamen dicitur aliquid possibile alicui quia aliquis potest super ipsum. Cum ergo dicit quod posse creari est alterius potentiae [61a] contra posse creare, si posse creari proprie dicatur quod sit posse subiecti creabilis, verum est, sed tunc

13. Reply to the thirteenth objection: in whatever sense "prior" is taken, the following is false: "the *non-esse* of the world was prior to its *esse*." This, however, is true: "the *esse* of the world was not prior." The reason is that, as was touched upon above, by saying "the *non-esse* of the world was prior" we predicate a measure which has of necessity "before" and "after" with respect to time, because every measure which has a temporal priority also has something subsequent to itself inasmuch as here there is question of priority in extension.

14–15. Replies to objections fourteen and fifteen: affirmation and negation concern the same subject, not as being, but as apprehended by the intellect. For a thing, insofar as it is apprehended by the intellect, is apprehended without regard to either its *esse* or its *non-esse*. For it is not its own *esse*. Hence something is common to both, not in the real order, but insofar as it is related to the intellect. Even then, the element is common, not as being, but as capable of being grasped by the intellect. The answer to the fifteenth objection is evident.

16. Reply to the sixteenth objection: when it is said, "everything which comes to be could come to be," I make a distinction: if we are talking about something in the course of nature, then it can come to be according to the course of nature; if, however, we are talking about something above the course of nature, it can come to be by a power above nature, that is, by the power of the Creator, which with respect to things intrinsic to it is always conjoined with its act, but with respect to things extrinsic to it, not at all.

17. Reply to the seventeenth objection: this is already evident since what is said is true of an interior act but is false of an exterior act.

18. Reply to the eighteenth objection: something is properly said to be possible according to the potency in that thing. In a broad sense, something is said to be possible for someone when that someone has power over it. Consequently, when it is said that "to be able to be created" belongs to another potency distinct from "to be able to create," then, if we are talking about "to be able to be created" in the proper sense, i.e., as the

posse creari nihil est. Si autem posse creari dicatur secundum rationem, quia Creator potest super creabile, tunc idem est posse creari et creare. Quod autem dicitur quod posse creari non dicitur de Creatore, verum est quantum ad modum loquendi; secundum rem tamen diceretur de ipso.

19. Ad decimum nonum dicendum quod potentiae differunt sicut termini quando secundum veritatem sunt diversae potentiae. Sed in proposito una est Dei potentia naturae mancipata a qua possunt esse diversi effectus.

20. Ad vigesimum dicendum quod creare non est agere, sed facere. Unde Augustinus, *De Trinitate* V, cap. 11:[42] "Quod autem ad faciendum attinet, de solo Deo verissime dicitur." Facere igitur non [requirit] in quid agat. — Aliter autem loquitur Philosophus[43] de agere et facere, vocans actilia quorum finis est in ipsa operatione, sicut [in] actu cytharizandi et opere virtutis de quibus nihil relinquitur post factum. Factilia sunt quae post operationem manent, ut aedificia et consimilia. Unde dicit Philosophus quod prudentia est habitus vera ratione activus; ars vero habitus vera ratione factivus. — Item, de his aliter loquitur Augustinus, *Contra adversarium legis*, cap. 15,[44] dicens: "Facere est quod omnino non erat; creare autem, ex eo quod iam erat ordinando aliquid constituere; ideoque dictus est Deus creans mala."

21. Ad vigesimum primum dicendum quod aliud est de causa materiali, quae omnino est imperfectionis et in Deum nullo modo cadere non [sic!] potest, aliud de aliis causis.

---

[42] More correctly, c. 8, n. 9 (PL 42, 917; CCL 50, 216).
[43] Cf. *Ethic. Nic.* VI, c. 4 (1140a 1–24); then below, for the distinction between prudence and art, *Ethic. Nic.* VI, c. 4, and c. 7 (1140a 9-10; 1141b 22).
[44] Book I, c. 23, n. 48 (PL 42, 633); cf. St. Thomas, *Summa theol.* I, 45, 1, arg. 1 (283b 29-32). Cf. Isaiah 45. 7.

capacity of a subject which can be created, it is true. But then "to be able to be created" is nothing. But if we are talking about "to be able to be created" as a merely rational distinction, since the Creator has power over what can be created, then "to be able to be created" and "to be able to create" are the same. But when it is said that "to be able to be created" is not predicated of the Creator, this is true insofar as this is a way of speaking; but as indicating what is really the case, it would be said of Him.

19. Reply to the nineteenth objection: potencies differ as their termini when they are truly diverse potencies. But in the present case God's potency is one given over to nature from which diverse effects can come to be.

20. Reply to the twentieth objection: "to create" is not "to act" but "to make." Thus Augustine in *De Trinitate* V, ch. 11, says: "But what pertains to making is said most truly of God alone." To make, therefore, does not act on something. The Philosopher, however, speaks of "to act" and "to make" in another way when he calls those things "*actilia*" whose end is in the operation itself, just as in the act of playing the zither or in an act of virtue where nothing of them remains after they are done. "*Factilia*" are those things which remain after the operation, such as buildings and the like. Thus the Philosopher says that prudence is truly an "active" habit, while art is truly a "factive" habit. Again, Augustine in *Contra adversarium legis*, ch. 15, speaks of these things in another way: "to make is to produce something which was in no way at all; but to create is to constitute something by ordering what already was; and so God is said to create evils."

21. Reply to the twenty-first objection: it is one thing in the case of a material cause which is altogether imperfect and so can in no way at all be in God; it is something quite different in the case of the other causes.

22. Ad vigesimum secundum dicendum quod eductum educebatur quando erat, quia simul educebatur et eductum est. Et cum dicitur: 'quod erat non indiget Creatore,' verum est de eo quod est post acceptionem esse; sed de eo quod accipit esse simul et creationem,[45] non est verum.

23. Ad vigesimum tertium dicendum est quod creatio actio non dicit actionem Dei intrinsecam tantum, sed coniunctionem eius cum effectu exteriori quem connotat communicatio[46] quae simul est cum creato. — Ad obiectum quod actio non est sine termino actionis, dicendum quod verum est. Tamen aliter est in actione divina quae est tota causa acti, aliter in aliis.

24. Ad vigesimum quartum dicendum quod non est simile de potentia creabilis et de potentia numeri, non ratione subiecti potentiae nec ratione termini, quia potentia creabilis est in creante, iuxta illud Augustini, *Ad Volusianum*:[47] "In rebus mutabilibus tota ratio [facti] est potentia facientis." Item, nec ratione termini, quia creabile ordinatur ad actum purum, potentia autem numeri ad actum mixtum cum potentia, quia unus numerus via est ad alium.

25. Ad vigesimum quintum dicendum . . .[48]

---

45 Highly conjectural; *cu* in **F**.
46 communicatio (conject.)] concreatio **F** (with cross above it).
47 *Epist*. 137, c. 2, n. 8 (PL 33, 519, CSEL 44, 107).
48 Lacuna at this point of some twelve lines.

22. Reply to the twenty-second objection: since the "was being educed" and "what was educed" are simultaneous, what was educed was educed at the time the thing was. And when it is said that what was does not need a Creator," this is true of what is, after having received *esse*; but it is not true of what receives *esse* at the time it is created.

23. Reply to the twenty-third objection: creation as *actio* does not say merely an intrinsic action of God but also His conjunction with an exterior effect, which communication connotes as being simultaneous with what is created. To the objection that *actio* is not without a terminus of the action, it must be said that this is true. But it is true in one way in the divine *actio* which is the total cause of what is done and in another way in other things.

24. Reply to the twenty-fourth objection: there is no comparison between the capacity to be created and the capacity for number, either because of the subject of the potency or because of its terminus, since the capacity to be created is in the Creator according to Augustine in *Ad Volusianum*: "In changeable things the entire explanation of what is made is the potency of the maker." Again, it is not because of its terminus, since what can be created is ordered to pure act, while the capacity for number is ordered to act mixed with potency inasmuch as one number leads to another.

25. Reply to the twenty-fifth objection: . . .

II

Utrum mundus potuit fieri ab aeterno.[1]
Quaeritur, hoc supposito, si[2] mundus potuit ab aeterno creari.
Et ostenditur quod sic:

1. Quia dicit Dionysius, *De divinis nominibus:*[3] "Bonum est sui diffusivum." Et Augustinus, *Contra adversarium legis:*[4] "Istorum producendorum causa sola bonitas Dei fuit." Ergo sicut simul sunt lux et diffusio lucis, sic bonum et diffusio bonitatis. Sed bonum fuit ab aeterno, ergo et diffusio eius quae est creatio.

2. Item, Augustinus, *De Trinitate* VI, cap. 1:[5] "Est coaeternus Patri Filius, sicut splendor qui gignitur ab igne atque diffunditur coaevus[6] est illi, et esset aeternus, si ignis[7] esset aeternus."[F 61b]. Si igitur ignis a se habet effectum diversum sibi coaevum, ergo et Deus potest. — Respondebatur[8] quod creatura non potest capere aeternitatem. — [3.] Contra: Augustinus, *Ad Volusianum:*[9] "In rebus artificialibus[10] [L 97b] tota ratio facti est potentia facientis." Sed creatio est operatio summe mirabilis; ergo totaliter dependet a potentia Dei. Ergo nulla impotentia repugnat a parte recipientis.

4. Item, quando creatura non est, nihil potest recipere quantum est a parte sui, nec esse nec aeternum esse, quia a pari est impossibilitas ad utrumque. Ergo qua ratione potest recipere unum et reliquum.

---

[1] Title taken from the list of questions, F., f. 19c.
[2] hic supposito si] utrum L.
[3] Cf. *De divinis nominibus,* c. 4, n. 1 (PG 3, 693; *Dionysiaca* I, 146); the axiom is more derived than direct (*ut exverbis Dionysii accipitur,* remarks St. Thomas, *Summa theologiae* I, 5, 4, arg. 2; 30a 2). On its use in Scholasticism before St. Thomas, cf. J. G. Bougerol, "Saint Bonaventure et le Pseudo-Denys l'Aréopagite," *Études franciscaines* 19 (1969), suppl. annuel, 81–104.
[4] Book I, c. 7, n. 10 (PL 42, 609).
[5] PL 42, 923; CCL 50, 228; cf. P. Lombard, *Sent.* I, d. 9, c. 2, n. 3 (ed. cit., 103–104).
[6] coaevus] coeternus L.
[7] ignis . . . Si *om.* (homoioleuton) L.
[8] Respondebatur F, respondetur L.
[9] *Epist.* 137, c. 2, n. 8 (PL 33, 519, CSEL 44, 107).
[10] artificialibus F, mirabilibus L, talibus *Aug.*

II

On this supposition the question is whether the world could have been made from eternity.

It is shown that the answer is affirmative:

1. Because in the *De divinis nominibus* Dionysius says: "The Good gives of itself." And Augustine in *Contra adversarium legis* says: "The sole cause of their production was the goodness of God." Consequently, just as light and its diffusion are simultaneous, so too are good and its diffusion. But the good was from eternity and, therefore, so was its diffusion, i.e., its creation.

2. Again, Augustine in *De Trinitate* VI, ch. 1, says: "The Son is coeternal with the Father in the same way as brightness, generated and diffused by fire, is coeval with the fire, and it would be eternal if the fire were eternal." Hence, if fire of itself has a coeval effect distinct from itself, so can God. It was said in reply that a creature cannot take hold of eternity.

3. To the contrary, Augustine in *Ad Volusianum* says: "In artifacts the entire explanation of what is made is the power of the maker." But creation is the most wonderful operation; it depends, therefore, totally on God's power. Consequently, no lack of power on the part of the recipient is inconsistent with it.

4. Further, when a creature does not exist, it can receive nothing from itself, neither *esse* nor eternal *esse*, since both are equally impossible. By the same token, therefore, if it can receive the one, it can receive the other.

5. Item, plus potest Deus de nihilo quam creatura de aliquo. Sed si ignis fuisset ab aeterno, genuisset splendorem suum ab aeterno, ut dicit Augustinus.[11] Ergo Deus potuit ab aeterno producere mundum[12] de nihilo.

6. Item[13] posita causa sufficienti, ponitur effectus. Sed Deus est causa mundi solus et sufficiens. Sed haec causa fuit aeterna; ergo et creatum. — Respondebatur[14] ad hoc argumentum quod non sequitur de causa[15] voluntarie agente, quia eius effectus est secundum modum voluntatis suae. — [7.] Contra: ergo si voluisset ab aeterno mundum produxisse, potuisset. — Respondetur quod verum est quantum est ex parte sui. — [8.] Contra: Deus quantum est ex parte sui nihil potest nisi quod posse esse est possibile,[16] cum 'posse' dicat respectum ad obiectum potentiae. Ergo, si Deus potuit ab aeterno mundum producere quantum est ex se, mundus potuit ab aeterno produci.

9. Item, aeque potens Deus est producere finitum sicut infinitum. Sed produxit ab aeterno infinitum, scilicet Filium suum. Ergo et potuit[17] ab aeterno producere finitum.

10. Item, mundus non incepit esse; ergo fuit ab aeterno. Probatio primae: si incepit esse aut in tempore aut in instanti. Non in tempore, quia inter ens et non-ens non est medium. Ergo incepit in instanti. Sed hoc est impossibile; ergo non incepit. Quod sit impossibile,[18] probatur: quia eadem est ratio de mundi inceptione et eius desitione. Mundus autem si desineret, non desineret in instanti.

---

[11] Above in arg. 2.
[12] mundum *trp. after* potuit L.
[13] Cf. St. Thomas, *Summa theol.* I, 46, 1, arg. 9 (294a 11–20).
[14] Respondebatur F, respondetur L. — Cf. St. Thomas, ibid., ad 9 (295a 47–296a 5).
[15] de causa *om.* L.
[16] est possibile L, posuit F (with a cross in margin).
[17] potuit F, est possibile L.
[18] ergo . . . impossibile *om.* (*hom.*) L.

5. Again, God can do more with nothing than a creature can with something. But if fire were from eternity, it would have generated its brightness from eternity, as Augustine says. God, therefore, could produce the world from eternity out of nothing.

6. Further, once a sufficient cause is posited so are its effects. But God is the sole and sufficient cause of the world. But this cause was eternal; so, therefore, is what was created. The reply to this argument was that it does not follow in the case of a cause acting voluntarily because its effect is according to the manner of its willing.

7. To the contrary: it follows, then, that if He had willed to have produced the world from eternity, He could have done so. In reply it may be said that this is true to the extent that it depends on the agent.

8. To the contrary: God, to the extent that it is up to Him, can do nothing except what is really possible, since "to be able" implies a relation to the object of a potency. Insofar as God is concerned, therefore, if He could produce the world from eternity, the world could have been made from eternity.

9. Further, God is equally able to produce something finite as something infinite. But He produced something infinite from eternity, namely, His Son. Hence He could also have produced something finite from eternity.

10. Again, the world did not begin to be; therefore it was from eternity. Proof of the first part: if the world began to be, it did so either in time or in an instant. It did not begin in time because between being and non-being there is no middle ground. Hence it began in an instant. But this is impossible; consequently, it did not begin. Its impossibility is proved thus: the explanation of the world's beginning is the same as that of its ending. But if the world were to cease, it would not cease in an instant.

11. Hoc probatur sic: quia si mundus verteretur in nihilum, mundus in sua annihilatione non esset, et annihilatio mundi esset terminus sui[19] esse. Sed mensura annihilationis esset cum annihilatione, sicut mensura omnis motus est cum motu et mutationis cum mutatione. Ergo si annihilatio est in instanti, instans est cum annihilatione. Sed annihilatio est[20] post esse mundi; ergo et instans quod est eius mensura. Ergo, si mundus annihilatur in instanti, instans est[21] post esse mundi. Sed hoc est impossibile, cum pars non sit sine toto, nec accidens sine subiecto; ergo etc. — Respondebatur[22] quod anihilatio est in nunc aeternitatis. — Contra: Quidquid est in nunc aeternitatis est aeternum. Sed annihilatio illa, hoc[23] casu posito, non esset aeterna; ergo etc.

12. Item, si mundus non potest esse aeternus, hoc non nisi quia habet esse post non-esse. Quod[24] est falsum; ergo primum. Quod non habeat esse post non-esse probatur: quia nec post secundum[25] naturam, cum non-esse non dicat materiam.[26] — Item, quia prius tantum natura simul est tempore cum posteriori, sicut materia cum forma. Nec prius tempore, quia non prius erat tempus;[27] nec prius aeternitate, quia non-esse mundi non fuit in aeternitate. Sic enim non-esse vel nihil esse esset in perfectissimo esse [L 97c] et negatio in affirmatione purissima; ergo etc.

13. Item, praeteritum et futurum sunt aequalia in suppositis. Quidquid enim est praeteritum, fuit futurum; et quidquid est futurum erit praeteritum. Ergo, qua ratione est unum infinitum, et reliquum est vel esse poterit infinitum.

---

[19] sui *om.* F.
[20] est *om.* F.
[21] est F, autem L.
[22] Respondebatur L, respondetur F.
[23] hoc *om.* L.
[24] Quod F, sed hoc L.
[25] secundum *om.* F.
[26] materiam F, naturam L.
[27] tempus F, tempore L.

11. Proof: because, if the world were to turn into nothingness, it would not exist in the moment of its annihilation, and the annihilation of the world would be the terminus of its *esse*. But then the measuring of annihilation would be simultaneous with the annihilation itself, just as the measuring of all motions is simultaneous with motion and of change with change. Hence, if annihilation is in an instant, the instant is simultaneous with the annihilation. But annihilation comes after the world's *esse*, and therefore, so does the instant which is its measure. Consequently, if the world is annihilated in an instant, that instant is after the world's *esse*. But this is impossible, since there can be no part without the whole, and no accident without a subject; therefore, etc. It was replied that annihilation is in the now of eternity. Whatever is in the now of eternity is eternal. But such an annihilation, supposing that it happened, would not be eternal; therefore, etc.

12. Further, if the world cannot be eternal, this is only because it has *esse* after *non-esse*. But the consequent is false; therefore so is the antecedent. That the world may not have *esse* after *non-esse* is proved thus: *esse* is not "after" by nature, since *non-esse* does not say matter, and again, since what is prior only by nature is temporally simultaneous with what is posterior, e.g., matter with form. *Non-esse* is not prior in time because before *esse* there was no time. *Non-esse* is not prior in eternity because the world's *non-esse* is not in eternity. If it were, then *non-esse* or *esse nihil* would be in the most perfect being, and a negation would be in the purest affirmation; therefore, etc.

13. Again, past and future are equals in their supposits. For whatever is past was future; and whatever is future will be past. For the very same reason, therefore, that the one is infinite, the other is or can be infinite in the future.

14. Item, Boethius, *De consolatione* V:[28] "Neque Deus conditis[29] rebus antiquior videri debet. Ergo Deus non est antiquior mundo: ergo si Deus aeternus, et mundus.

15. Item, in habentibus materiam quod est ab agente per artem est secundum modum agentis, quantum patitur conditio materiae. Ergo quod est ab alio[30] sine materia, est totaliter secundum modum agentis. Sed mundus sensibilis exprimitur a mundo architypo sine praeiacente materia: ergo est[31] secundum modum agentis omnino. Ergo, si mundus architypus vel exemplaris est aeternus, et mundus [F 61c] iste sensibilis erit aeternus.

16. Item, Deus[32] est agens naturale et voluntarium. Si igitur produxit de novo[33] mundum: aut in quantum agens naturale vel per principium quod est natura, aut per principium quod est voluntas. Si primo modo: sed natura agit uniformiter et determinate unum. Ergo aut ab aeterno produxit, aut nunquam produxit. Si autem produxit in quantum agens voluntarium: sed non est impotentior natura quam voluntas. Ergo ab aeterno potuit producere sicut si[34] ex natura produxisset.

17. Item, quod non repugnet conditio[ni] creaturae produci ab aeterno, probatur: quoniam dicendo mundum creatum fuisse ab aeterno, duo dico: et mundum semper fuisse, et semper ab alio esse habuisse. Sed[35] in hoc si aliquid repugnat rationi creaturae, quaero: aut quia potentia esse ab alio aeternaliter, et hoc non,[36] quia Filius est ab aeterno; aut quia potentia[37] ab aeterno diversitate substantiae, et hoc non, quia si

---

[28] Prosa 6 (PL 63, 859 B; CCL 94, 101).
[29] conditis] conditor **L**.
[30] alio **F**, aliquo **L**.
[31] est *om.* **F**.
[32] Deus *om.* **F**.
[33] de novo **L**, deus **F**.
[34] si *om.* **F**.|| produxisset **L**, potuisset **F**.
[35] Sed *om.* **F**.
[36] non] est *add.* **F**.
[37] potentia **L**, est **F**.

14. Further, Boethius in *De consolatione* V says: "God ought not to seem older than created things. Hence God is not older than the world; consequently, if God is eternal, so is the world."

15. Again, in material things what an agent makes through art exists after the manner of the agent to the extent that the condition of matter allows. What comes from an agent without [pre-existing] matter, therefore, exists totally after the manner of the agent. But the sensible world is expressed by an archetypal world without any pre-existing matter; hence it exists completely after the manner of the agent. Consequently, if the archetypal or exemplary world is eternal, then this sensible world will be eternal also.

16. Further, God is a natural and voluntary agent. If, therefore, He made the world anew, He did so either as a natural agent (or through a principle which is nature), or through a principle which is will. Suppose He did it in the first way: since nature does one thing uniformly and with determinateness, then either He produced the world from eternity or He never produced it. But suppose He made it as a voluntary agent. But nature is not less powerful than will.[5] Hence He could have made the world from eternity just as if He had made it out of nature.

17. Again, that it is not contradictory for a creature to be made from eternity is proved as follows: when I say that the world had been created from eternity, I say two things: (1) the world always was, and (2) it always had *esse* from another. But if there is anything in this which contradicts the meaning of being a creature, I ask: (1) whether it is the capacity to have *esse* from another eternally (and this is not so because the Son is from eternity), or (2) whether it is because the possibility of there being diverse substances from eternity is contradictory

---

[5] Although this is how our Latin text has it, one wonders whether Pecham should have said, "But will is not less powerful than nature."

caelum fuisset ab aeterno motus fuisset aeternus, qui tamen essentialiter differt a caelo;[38] aut quia in hoc aequipararetur Deo,[39] et hoc non, quia aeternitas eius esset aeternitati Dei incomparabilis, cum haberet partem post partem; et sicut modo esset duratio mundi successiva cum simplici aeternitate Dei, sic potuisset, ut videtur, si ab aeterno fuisset.

18. Item, si Deus produxit mundum ex tempore proposito aeterno, ergo[40] mutatus est implendo propositum. Probatio consequentiae:[41] quia quod voluit ab aeterno producere, productum actu voluit. Causa autem aut[42] fuit a parte mundi; et hoc non videtur, quia mundus cum produceretur nullam habuit[43] causam suae productionis; aut fuit a parte Dei, et ita Deus implendo ex tempore quod ab aeterno disposuit, mutatus est.

19. Item, res habent comparationem ad causam materialem et efficientem. Sed materiatum potest esse coaevum[44] materiae sicut cantus sono; ergo et efficienti. Probatio: nihil fit[45] de materia nisi cum mutatione materiae. Sed quod fit a Deo, fit sine mutatione Dei vel etiam sine mutatione proprie dicta eius quod est sic, quia creatio non est mutatio proprie dicta.[46] Ergo magis potest aliquid creatum[47] coaeternum esse creanti quam materiae de qua est.

20. Item, Deus dat creaturae aliquid mediantibus principiis suis, aliquid sine concursu alicuius principii, sicut in creatione. [L 97d] Sed dat creaturae perpetuitatem sui esse quia convenit suis principiis a parte post. Ergo potest eidem dare aeternitatem a parte ante quam dat mediantibus principiis.

---

[38] celum eternum implicat opposita *marg. note* F[2].
[39] Deo *om* F.
[40] ergo *om.* L.
[41] consequentiae L, consequentis F.
[42] Causa autem aut F, tamen causa L.
[43] habuit F, haberet L.
[44] coaevum] corporeum F (marked by cross).
[45] fit F, est L.
[46] mutatio proprie dicta L, proprie mutatio F.
[47] creatum *om.* F ‖ coaeternum esse *trp.* L.

(and this is not so since, if the heavens had been from eternity, their motion, which nonetheless differs essentially from the heavens, would have been eternal), or (3) whether it is because creatures would in this way be equal to God (and this is not so since the creature's eternity would be incomparable to God's, because it would have part following upon part); and just as now the successive duration of the world would be compatible with God's simple eternity, so, it would seem, the creature could have been "equal" to God, if it had been from eternity.

18. Further, if God made the world from an eternity of time as is proposed, then God is changed in implementing the proposal. Proof of the inference: Whatever God willed to produce from eternity, that product He actually willed to exist. The cause of this production was either in the world or in God. It does not seem to be in the world, since, when the world was produced, it had no cause of its own production. If it was in God, then, by implementing in time what He had planned from eternity, God was changed.

19. Again, things have a relation to a material and to an efficient cause. But what is made of matter can be coeval with matter just as song is coeval with sound; hence what is made of matter can also be coeval with its efficient cause. Proof: nothing is made out of matter without a change in matter. But what is made by God is made without a change in God or even a change in the proper sense in what is so made, because creation is not properly speaking a change. All the more, therefore, can something created be coeternal with the Creator than with the matter out of which it is made.

20. Further, certain things God gives to the creature through the mediation of its own nature; other things He gives without such help, as in creation. But He gives the creature an uninterrupted continuation of its *esse*, because this is in accord with its nature relative to the future. God, therefore, can give it eternity relative to the past, and He gives it this eternity through the mediation of its nature.

21. Item, productio creaturae ex tempore causam habet solùm Dei voluntatem. Sed quod[48] ex sola causa tali pendet, ipsa sola mutari potest. Ergo si Deus vellet, aliter esse posset vel fuisse potuisset.

22. Item, si mundus productus est in instanti, hoc non potest esse quia instans est copulatio[49] duorum temporum, et ita ante tempus esset tempus.

23. Item, inter processionem aeternam, quae est in identitae substantiae, et temporalem, quae est in diversitate essentiae, medium est: vel processio in identitate naturae ex tempore, vel processio in diversitate naturae ab aeterno. Primum est impossibile; ergo secundum est necessarium.[50]

24. Item, aut Deus ab aeterno potuit mundum producere, et voluit; aut potuit, sed noluit; aut voluit, sed non potuit. Si primum est verum, ergo produxit. Si secundum est verum,[51] ergo invidus fuit, sicut de generatione Filii arguit Augustinus.[52] Si tertium est verum, impotens fuit. Sed haec duo ultima sunt impossibilia; ergo primum est necessarium.

25. Item, potuit fuisse mundus mille annis antequam[53] fuit, per mille annos et iterum per mille, et sic in infinitum. Ergo potuit ab aeterno.

26. Item, *De ecclesiasticis dogmatibus* X:[54] "In principio creavit Deus omnia, ut non esset otiosa Dei bonitas." Ergo si non creavit ab aeterno, fuit otiosus ab aeterno.

---

[48] quod *om.* F.
[49] copulatio L, copula F.
[50] necessarium] quia semper alterum concomitatur (?) *marg. note* F[2].
[51] est verum *om.* F.
[52] "Deum quem genuit, quoniam meliorem se generare non potuit (nihil enim Deo melius), generare debuit aequalem. Si enim voluit, et non potuit, infirmus est; si potuit, et non voluit, invidus est. Ex quo conficitur aequalem genuisse Filium"; *De divers. Quaest.* 83, q. 50 (PL 40, 31s); cf. P. Lombard. *Sent.* I, d. 44, c. 1, n. 2 (ed. cit. 304).
[53] mundus . . . antequam F. mundura (?) priusquam L.
[54] Gennadius, *De eccl. dogm.* (PL 58, 983 C–D); the text is abbreviated.

21. Again, the production of a creature in time has God's will as its sole cause. But what depends solely on such a cause can be changed only by that cause. Hence, if God so willed, it could be or could have been otherwise.

22. Further, if the world was made in an instant, such a production is impossible, since an instant links two time intervals, and so there would be time before time.

23. Again, between eternal procession, which is within the identity of substance, and temporal procession, which is in the diversity of essence, there is a middle ground: namely, a temporal procession within the identity of nature or an eternal procession within the diversity of nature. The first is impossible; the second is, therefore, necessary.

24. Further, either God could have made the world from eternity and willed to do so, or He could have and did not will to do so, or He willed to do so, but could not so make the world. If the first, He did so make it. If the second, then, as Augustine argued concerning the generation of the Son, God was envious. If the third, God was powerless. But these last two are impossible; the first is, therefore, necessary.

25. Again, the world could have been a thousand years before it was, and a thousand before that, and a thousand before that, and so on indefinitely. Hence it could have been from eternity.

26. Further, in *De ecclesiasticis dogmatibus* X it is said: "In the beginning God created all things in order that God's goodness might not be idle." Hence, if God did not create from eternity, He was idle from eternity.

27. Item, Deus est causa rerum in triplici genere causae. Sed ad perfectionem exemplaris pertinet ut sit aeternum. Ergo ad perfectionem efficientis similiter.

28. Item, si mundus incepit in aliquo [F 61d] instanti, verbi gratia in A, ante A mundus non erat. Ante autem A, quando mundus non erat, dicatur B. Sed inter A et B, cum non sint simul, cadit[55] medium, et tempus per consequens. Ergo ante mundum[56] fuit tempus.

29. Item, si fit aliqua prima mutatio, sit A. Ergo cum A incepit, prius fuit verum dicere A non esse actu sed potentia. Sed quidquid exit de potentia in actum, exit per mutationem. Ergo ante primam mutationem[57] fuit mutatio.

30. Item, Augustinus videtur docere quod non sit impossibile mundum fuisse ab aeterno. Unde dicit, *De civitate* XI, cap. 4:[58] "Qui a Deo mundum factum fatentur, non eum temporis volunt habere sed suae creationis initium, ut modo quodam vix intelligibili semper sit factus." Haec Augustinus. Sed mundus iste est vix intelligibilis; ergo non impossibilis. Nullum enim Deo impossibile est intelligibile, cui *non* est[59] *impossibile omne verbum*, dicitur Lucae primo.

31. Item, Deus non creavit mundum nisi quia bonum est mundum esse. Sed melius est esse ab aeterno quam non ab aeterno, cum esse ab aeterno conveniat Deo; ergo etc.[60]

CONTRA:

a. Gen. 1, 1: *In principio creavit Deus caelum et terram.*[61] Et loquitur Moyses de principio temporis quod continuatur per dies inferius enumeratos in canone.[62]

---

[55] cadit] tempore *add.* L ‖ tempus] tempore L.
[56] mundum F, medium L.
[57] mutationem] non *add.* F.
[58] PL 41, 319; CSEL 40-1, 515; CCL 48, 324, quoted in part by St. Thomas, *Summa theol.* I, 46, 2 ad 1 (297b 1-4). — Below, Luke I, 37.
[59] est F, sit L, ‖ impossibile] apud deum *add.* L.
[60] Lacuna of two lines in F.
[61] et terram] etc. L. ‖ Et loquitur Moyses L, loquitur F.
[62] Again a lacuna of two lines in F.

27. Again, God is the cause of things according to three kinds of causality. But it belongs to the perfection of an exemplar that it be eternal. In a similar way, therefore, it also belongs to the perfection of an efficient cause.

28. Further, if the world began in some instant, say in A, then before A the world was not. But the "before A," when the world was not, let us call B. But between A and B, there is a middle ground because they are not simultaneous, and so there was time. Hence, before the world was, there was time.

29. Again, suppose there comes about a first change; call it A. Then, when A began, it was true before that to say that A was not an act but a potency. But whatever goes from potency to act does so by changing. Before the first change, therefore, there was change.

30. Further, Augustine seems to teach that it is not impossible that the world was from eternity. In *De civitate* XI, ch. 4, he says: "Those who confess that God made the world do not want it to have a beginning of time, but a beginning of its creation, so that the world, in some barely intelligible way, would always be in the making." These are Augustine's words. But such a world is "barely intelligible"; hence it is not impossible. For nothing impossible to God is intelligible, for Whom "no word is impossible," as Luke says in the first chapter.

31. Again, God created the world only because it was good that the world exist. But it is better to exist from eternity than not to exist from eternity, since to exist from eternity is proper to God; therefore, etc.

To the Contrary:

a. Genesis 1.1: "In the beginning God created heaven and earth." And Moses speaks of a beginning of time which is continued through the days enumerated further on in the text.

b. Item contra:[63] Avicenna VI *Metaphysicae*:[64] "Postquam res [L 98a] ex seipsa[65] habet non-esse, sequitur tunc ut eius esse sit post non-esse et fiat postquam non fuerat."

c. Item, mensura est per quod[66] cognoscitur quantitas. Ergo quae est actio duarum invicem quantitatum, eadem erit proportio invicem mensurarum suarum. Deus habet quantitatem virtutis, mundus habet quantitatem molis.[67] Sed non est aliqua quantitas creaturae quae posset commensurari[68] quantitati vel magnitudini divinae. Deus enim ita est in hoc mundo quod posset esse in mundo alio;[69] si etiam esset maior in infinitum, nec etiam[70] posset facere mundum sibi conproportionalem. Ergo nec duratio mundi potest ex aliqua parte aequari aeternitati.[71] Sed aequaretur si esset factus ab aeterno. Ergo impossibile est Deum creasse mundum ab aeterno.

d. Item, si mundus creatus est non in tempore, quia inter esse et non-esse purum non est medium, ergo creatus est in instanti; quaero: aut instanti initiali temporis aut mediali[72] aut finali, cum non sit aliud cogitare. Tertium est manifeste falsum; similiter et secundum, quia tunc tempus fuisset ante mundum. Ergo creatus est in instanti temporis[73] initiali. — Quod etiam patet per aliam viam. Cum enim creatio dedit mundo esse, ergo instans creationis fuit terminus essendi ipsi mundo a parte ante. Sed nihil huiusmodi[74] est vel esse potest aeternum; ergo etc.

---

[63] contra *om.* L.;
[64] Chapt. 1 (f. 91c).
[65] seipsa] se L.
[66] quod F, quam L.
[67] Cf Augustinus, *De Trin.* VI, 7(PL 42, 929, CCL 50, 237); in P. Lombard, *Sent.* I, d. 8, c. 4, n. 3 (ed. cit. 99).
[68] posset commensurari F, possit mensurari L.
[69] alio *om.* F.
[70] etiam *om.* F.
[71] aeternitati] trinitati F.
[72] initiali ... mediali *trp.* both FL.
[73] temporis *om.* F.
[74] huiusmodi F, tale L.

b. Again to the contrary. Avicenna in VI *Metaphysics* says: "When a thing has *non-esse* of itself, then it follows that its *esse* is after *non-esse* and it comes to be after it had not been."

c. Further, measure is that by which quantity is known. Consequently, whatever action there is between two quantities, the proportion will be the same. God has a quantity of power; the world has a quantity of mass. But no quantity in a creature could be commensurate with the quantity or magnitude of God. For God is in this world in such a way that He could have been in some other world even if that world were infinitely greater than this one. God could not make a world proportionate to Himself. Hence neither can the world's duration be equal to eternity in any way. But it would be equal to eternity if it had been made from eternity. It is impossible, therefore, for God to have created the world from eternity.

d. Again, if the world was not created in time, since between *esse* and pure *non-esse* there is no middle ground, then it was created in an instant. Now I ask: Was it created in the first instant of time or in some instant within time or in the last instant of time, since no other instant can be conceived? The third alternative is clearly false, and so is the second, since then there would have been time before the world. Consequently, the world was created in the first instant of time. This is evident in still another way. For, since creation gave the world *esse*, it follows that the instant of creation was the terminus of the world's very being in the past. But nothing of this sort is or can be from eternity; therefore, etc.

e. Item, si mundus duraverit per tempus infinitum et duraturus est similiter per tempus infinitum, tantumdem ergo[75] durabit quantum duraverit et non plus. Ergo[76] sicut non impediente infinitate praeteriti temporis[77] totum tempus praeteriit sic ut nihil eius sit futurum, similiter non obstante infinitate temporis futuri aliquando sic erit praeteritum ut nihil eius sit futurum. Sed[78] illud cum aliquando nihil erit futurum, penitus desinet. Ergo tempus est infinitum futurum et tamen aliquando deficiet omnino, quod est impossibile.

f. Item, creatio et versio opponuntur, quia creatio incipit a non-esse sicut versio terminatur in non-esse.[79] Item, versio respicit futurum sicut creatio[80] praeteritum. Ergo sicut impossibile est mundum verti in nihilum et tamen durare in infinitum a parte post, ita impossibile est mundum eductum fuisse de nihilo et[81] tamen durasse per tempus infinitum a parte ante.

g. Item, si mundus duravit per tempus infinitum et durabit[82] similiter, accipiatur ergo instans [F 62a] mediae diei, quod sit A; dicaturque totum tempus praeteritum A-praeteritum, et omne tempus futurum[83] A-futurum. Similiter sumatur aliud instans mediae diei, quod sit B; dicaturque totum tempus[84] praeteritum B-praeteritum, et totum futurum B-futurum. Item,[85] hiis positis, supponatur quod duorum aequalium quidquid est maius uno et reliquo, et quocumque unum est maius, et reliquum. Item supponatur quod quidquid sustinet alterum cum alio superaddito sit maius ipso vel totum ad[86] ipsum. Item, quod duo infinita ab eodem[87] indivisibili procedentia[88] sint aequalia. Ex hoc sic: A-praeteritum et A-futurum [L 98b] sunt aequalia, cum unum per impossibile alteri suppositum nec[89] excedat ipsum nec excedatur ab eo. Similiter B-praeteritum et B-futurum sunt aequalia. Sed B-praeteritum est

---

[75] tantumdem ergo L, ergo tantum F. ‖ et non plus om. L.
[76] Ergo] est ut videtur corruptum exemplar marg. note F2.
[77] praeteritii temporis om. F. ‖ praeteriit sic L, preteritum F.
[78] Sed corr. to Si F2. ‖ cum L, tamen F.
[79] The whole sentence is omitted in L.
[80] creatio] respicit add. L.
[81] et] tempus add. L.
[82] duraverit ... durabit F, durabit ... duravit L. ‖ similiter om. L.
[83] A-praeteritum ... futurum om. (hom.) L.
[84] tempus om. F.
[85] Item] ex add. F. ‖ supponatur ab eo F, supponitur L.
[86] ad om. L.
[87] eodem om. L.
[88] procedentia] precedentia F.
[89] nec F, non L. ‖ excedatur ab eo F, ab ipso excedatur L.

e. Further, if the world lasted through an infinite length of time, and, similarly, will last through an infinite length of time, then it will last just exactly as long as it will have lasted and no longer. Hence, just as the infinite length of past time does not prevent the whole of time from having lapsed in such a way that it has no future, in like manner the infinite length of future time does not prevent it from becoming past at some time or other in such a way that there is no future. But since at some time or other there will be no future, it will completely cease to be. Time, therefore, has an infinite future and, nonetheless, at some time or other will completely cease; but this is impossible.

f. Again, creation and destruction are opposed because creation begins from *non-esse*, while destruction terminates in *non-esse*. Further, destruction looks to the future, while creation looks to the past. Hence, just as it is impossible for the world to be turned into nothing and still last for an infinite time to come, so too is it impossible for the world to have been educed from nothing and still have lasted for an infinite time in the past.

g. Further, if the world will have lasted and will continue to last through an infinite time, then let us take an instant in the middle of the day, say A. Let us call the entire time gone by "past-A" and the entire time to come "future-A." In like manner, let us pick some other instant in the middle of the day, say B. Let us call the entire time gone by "past-B" and the entire time to come "future-B." Over and above these suppositions, let us also assume that whichever of two equals is greater than some other one is also greater than the other, and that by however much one is greater, by that much the other one is greater. Further, let us suppose that whichever supports the other with something extra added is either greater than it or is a whole relative to it. What is more, let us suppose that two infinities that proceed from the same indivisible point are equal. It then follows: A-past and A-future are equal since, if, *per impossibile*, one is superimposed on the other, the one would neither exceed nor be exceeded by the other. In like manner, B-past and B-future are equal. But B-past is greater than A-past and is

maius quam A-praeteritum, et totum ad ipsum. Ergo est maius quam A-futurum. Sed B-praeteritum et B-futurum sunt aequalia. Ergo B-futurum est maius quam A-futurum; sed A-futurum est totum ad B-futurum. Ergo pars est maior suo toto, posito quod tempus fuerit[90] sine initio.

h. Item, omne esse est aliquod bonum, et duratio maior est[91] melior minore. Ergo infinite maior, infinite melius alio. Ergo impossibile est aliquod creatum infinito tempore durasse.

i. Item, mundus duravit duratione infinita; sed mundus est propter hominem; ergo infiniti homines praecesserunt. Cum[92] ergo animae rationales sint immortales, sunt actu infinitae. Forte hoc non habebit pro inconvenienti qui volet contrarium sustinere. Sed contra: Infinita esse actu est omni philosophiae contrarium.[93] — Aliter docet alius haereticus animas interire cum corpore, quod est contra omnes nobiles philosophos; vel dicit omnium hominum esse animam unam, quod est contra rectissimam philosophiam, quae formam propriam dicit esse propriae materiae et unum esse motorem[94] unius mobilis; vel dicit quod animae successive revolvuntur in corpora diversa, et hoc a Philosopho improbatum et inter pythagoricas fabulas reputatum.[95]

---

[90] fuerit L, fuit F.

[91] est *om.* F.

[92] cum *trp. after* rationales F.

[93] Lacuna of three lines in F. — The whole argument is dependent on St. Bonaventure, *In II Sent.* d. 1, p. 1, a. 1, q. 2, fund. 5 (II, 21b); and to a lesser extent on St. Thomas, *Summa theol.* I, 46, 2, arg. 8 and ad 8 (296b 33–39; 298a 44–298a 17). Later in his so-called *Quodlibet Romanum* (that is, disputed at the Roman Curia), Pecham was to argue in Question V: "Item, si mundus fuisset ab aeterno, essent infinita actu, scilicet infinitae animae rationales, nisi ponatur animae interire cum corpore vel revolvi in corpora diversa: quorum quodlibet est impossibile theologiae et philosophiae [more likely: theologice et philosophice]"; ed. F. M. Delorme, *Joannis de Pecham Quodlibet Romanum* (Romae 1938), 17, 1–4.

[94] motorem L. mortem F (with cross in margin).

[95] *De anima* I, t. 53, c. 3 (407b 20–26).

a whole relative to it. Hence it is greater than A-future. But B-past and B-future are equal. B-future, therefore, is greater than A-future; but A-future is a whole relative to B-future. Consequently, the part is greater than its whole on the supposition that time had no beginning.

h. Again, every *esse* is something good, and a longer duration is better than a shorter. An infinitely longer duration, therefore, is infinitely better than the other. It is impossible, therefore, that some created thing has endured for an infinite time.

i. Further, the world lasted for an infinite time; but the world is for the sake of man; hence, in the past, there was an infinite number of men. Since, therefore, rational souls are immortal, there is an actual infinity of them. Perhaps this will not seem incongruous to those who wish to maintain the contrary. But to the contrary: that there be an actual infinity of things is contrary to every philosophy. Another heretic teaches something different when he says that souls perish with the body. But this is contrary to all noble Philosophers. Or another says that there is one soul for all men. But this is contrary to the most correct philosophy according to which there is a form proper to its own matter and one mover for each thing that can move. Or another says that souls are rotated successively from body to body. But this is rejected by the Philosopher and is held to be just another Pythagorean fable.

k. Item, Richardus, I *De Trinitate*, cap. 8,[96] dicit quod id quod est a seipso necessario est aeternum. Ergo per oppositum, quod non est a seipso est ex tempore; et loquor[97] de eo quod est ab alio essentialiter diverso. Haec consequentia sic probatur: quod est a seipso, eo ipso habet esse et esse posse; et quidquid aliud est ab ipso, ab ipso[98] participat esse et posse. Sed nullum participans ab altero aequatur in aliqua conditione illi quod participat. Ergo quod[99] participat recepit esse participatum ab eo quod est aeternum, [sed] non recipit ab aeterno. — Ad hoc respondetur[100] quod si mundus semper fuisset, non tamen Deo parificaretur, quia esse divinum est esse totum simul. — Contra: aequaretur suo modo, quia tantum durasset quantum[101] aeternitas Dei.

l. Item, omne pertransitum et acceptum est finitum. Ergo si omnes revolutiones caeli pertransitae sunt, sunt[102] finitae. — Ad hoc respondetur[103] quod transitus intelligitur a termino in terminum. Quaecumque autem praeterita dies signetur, finiti[104] sunt dies ab illa ad istam, et non oportet quod omnes sunt infiniti. — Contra: caelum pertransit revolutionem diurnam istam et aliam. Ergo si infinitae revolutiones praecesserunt, finitum transiit infinita, quod est contra rationem infiniti, [F 62b] cuius ratio est quod eius quantitatem accipientibus, semper est accipere aliquid extra.

m. Item, omne praeteritum fuit futurum. Totum tempus praeteritum est praeteritum.[105] Ergo totum tempus[106] fuit aliquando futurum. Sed quando totum fuit futurum, fuit in principio sui esse et durationis. Ergo omne tempus habuit initium suae durationis.

---

[96] PL 196, 894 D; ed. J. Ribailler, 93.
[97] loquor L, loquitur F.
[98] ab ipso *om.* L.
[99] quod F, si L.‖ participat] deficit *add.* L. ‖ recepit. . .recepit *om.* L.
[100] This is taken literally from St. Thomas, *Summa theologiae* I, 46, 2, ad 5 (298a 3–7).
[101] quantum L, sicut F.
[102] sunt *om.* F.
[103] From the *Summa theol.* I, 46, 2, ad 6 (298a 9–13).
[104] finiti F (and Thomas), finitae L. So also below.
[105] est praeteritum *om.* L.
[106] tempus *om.* L.

k. Again, Richard in I *De Trinitate*, ch. 8, says that what exists of itself is necessarily eternal. By *modus tollens*, therefore, what is not of itself is from time. I am speaking here of what is from another essentially diverse from itself. Proof of the consequence: what is of itself, by that very fact, has *esse* and the possibility of *esse*; and everything else is from it, i.e., shares in *esse* and possibility by its agency. But nothing that shares a perfection through the agency of another is equal in any way to what it shares in. Hence, what shares in *esse* receives the *esse* in which it shares from what is eternal, but it does not receive it from eternity. In reply it is said that, if the world had always been, still it would not be made equal to God since the divine *esse* is *esse* entire and simultaneous. To the contrary: in its own way it would be equal to God since it would have lasted as long as God's eternity.

l. Further, whatever is traversed and bounded is finite. Consequently, if all the turnings of the heavens have been gone through, they are finite. In reply it is said that "traversing" means going from one terminus to another. Whatever day in the past be chosen, from it to the other day there are a finite number of days, and it is not fitting for them all to be infinite. To the contrary: the heavens go through a revolution each day—this day and that day. Hence, if an infinite number of revolutions have already been gone through, then the finite traverses the infinite. But this contradicts the very meaning of the infinite, which is that, given a definite quantity, something more can always be added.

m. Again, every past was future. The entire time past is past. Hence, at some time or other all time was future. But when all time was future, it was at the beginning of its *esse* and duration. Every time, therefore, had a beginning of its duration.

n. Item, omne quod factum est, aliquando fuit in fieri. Sed mundus factus est. Ergo aliquando fuit in fieri, hoc est in aliquo instanti. Sed nullum instans [L 98c] distat ab instanti[107] infinite; ergo mundi creatio praecessit finite hoc instans.

o. Item, in causis efficientibus non est abire in infinitum. Ergo si pater est causa filii, non praecesserunt patres infiniti.[108] — Respondetur quod in causis per se ordinatis ad effectum aliquem non est abire in infinitum, sicut quod lapis moveretur a baculo et baculus a manu, et hoc in infinitum. Sed in efficientibus per accidens ordinatis non est impossibile; verbi gratia, accidit huic homini generare in quantum est genitus ab alio, quia generat in quantum homo, non inquantum genitus ab alio. — Contra: infinitas in causis accidentaliter ordinatis non potest esse nisi ab infinita virtute Creatoris. Cum igitur inter effectum istum signatum et Deum, qui est infinitus, simpliciter sint infiniti gradus causarum possibiles, non est ratio quare non possit esse[109] infinitas in causis ordinatis essentialiter sicut in ordinatis accidentaliter. — Item, ratio II *Metaphysicae*[110] videtur esse contra hoc. Et est talis: In agentibus ordinatis primum est causa medii et medium est causa ultimi, sive sit unum sive plura media. Remota autem causa, removetur illud cuius est causa. Remoto ergo primo, medium non potest esse cause Sed si procedatur in[111] causis efficientibus in infinitum, nulla causarum erit prima; ergo nulla erit secunda. Istud videtur sequi tam in causis essentialiter quam accidentaliter ordinatis.

p. Item, Philosophus, in fine . . .[112]

---

[107] instanti *om.* F.

[108] The argument is based on arg. 7 of the *Summa theol.* I, 46, 2 (296b 26–32). The response is rather literally from ad 7 (298a 16–43), with a mangled use of St. Thomas's own words.

[109] esse *om.* L.

[110] A-minor, t. 6, c. 2 (994a 11–18). Cf. St. Thomas, loc. cit. arg. 7.

[111] in L, a F.

[112] Lacuna of five lines in F; whole line omitted in L, which proceeds immediately to the Response.

n. Further, everything that was made, at some time or other was in the process of becoming. But the world was made. Consequently, at some time or other it was in the process of becoming, that is, it was in some instant. But no instant is infinitely far from another instant. The creation of the world, therefore, preceded this instant by a finite interval.

o. Again, there is no infinite regress in efficient causes. Hence, if even father is the cause of son, there was not an infinite number of fathers in the past. In reply it is said that in causes ordered essentially to an effect, there is no infinite regress as in the case of a stone moved by a stick, moved by a hand, and so on infinitely. But in efficient causes ordered accidentally to an effect, such a regress is not impossible; for example, it just happens that this man generates insofar as he was generated by another because he generates precisely as man and not precisely insofar as he is generated by another. To the contrary: an infinity in accidentally ordered causes can come only from the infinite power of the Creator. Since, therefore, between that designated effect and God, Who is infinite, there are simply an infinite number of possible degrees of causes, there is no reason why there could not be an infinite number of essentially as well as accidentally ordered causes. Further, the argument in II *Metaphysics* seems to be against this position. It goes like this: in ordered efficient causes the first in the series is cause of the in-between and the in-between is the cause of the last, whether there be one or many in-betweens. But take away the cause and the effect is taken away. Hence, take away the first and the in-between cannot be a cause. But if there be an infinite series of efficient causes, there will be no first among the causes; consequently, there will be no second. This seems to follow in the case of both essentially and accidentally ordered causes.

p. Further, the Philosopher, at the end . . .

RESPONSIO:

Creatio mundi ex tempore quamvis sit articulus fidei,[113] tamen ratione, ut videtur, potest investigari. Nec hoc est in praeiudicium fidei, dum non propter rationem fidei assentitur, sed merito fidei ad eius intelligentiam pervenitur. Unde qui sine fide de creatione locuti sunt, omnes erraverunt vel diminute,[114] non eam attribuendo Deo, vel superflue, attribuendo eam alii a Deo.

Mundum[115] igitur fuisse ex tempore et non ab aeterno creatum patet considerando primo in ipso veram praeteritionem fieri;[116] secundo participationem essendi; tertio modum suae originis; quarto mensuram suae productionis; quinto totum decursum temporis.

Prima ratio.[117] Primo dico, considerando praeteritionem ipsius fieri mundi, quoniam suum fieri vere transit in praeteritum. Omne autem praeteritum aliquando fuit praesens et non praeteritum. Nullum autem tale fuit ab aeterno. Ideo dicit Augustinus, *Super Genesim contra Manichaeum*:[118] "Non coaevum Deo mundum dicimus, non eius aeternitatis est mundus, cuius aeternitatis est Deus. Mundum quippe Deus fecit, et cum ipsa creatura quam Deus[119] fecit tempora esse coeperunt." Ergo si fecit, fieri transit in praeteritum quod est temporis initium.

---

[113] Cf. St. Thomas, loc. cit., sed contra, and resp.
[114] diminute L, dimitti (corr. *in* dimitte) sunt (= non?) F, *with* loquti sup. add. *marg.* F². ‖ non eam *trp.* L. ‖ superflue *om.* F. ‖ attribuendo] etiam *add.* F.
[115] Mundum F, Quemadmodum L.
[116] fieri F, fiendi L.
[117] Prima ratio *marg.* L, *om.* F (so also below).
[118] Book I, c. 2, n. 4 (PL 34, 175).
[119] Deus *om.* F.

SOLUTION:

The creation of the world in time, although it is an article of faith, can, it seems, still be investigated by reason. And this is not in prejudice of the faith, provided that assent is given to it not because of faith but rather we come to an understanding of it with the help of faith. Consequently, all of those who spoke about creation without faith erred either on the side of defect by not attributing it to God, or on the side of excess by attributing it to something other than God.

That the world was created in time, and not from eternity, is evident from a consideration first of the true passing into history of its coming-to-be; second, of its participation in being; third, of the way it began; fourth, of the measure of its production; and, fifth, of the entire lapse of time.

First Reason: In the first place, I say, by considering the passing into history of the world's coming-to-be, since its coming-to-be has truly gone into the past. But every past time was at some time or other present, and not past. But nothing like that was from eternity. Hence in *Super Genesim contra Manichaeum* Augustine says: "We do not say that the world was coeval with God, because the world does not have that eternity that is God's. Indeed God made the world, and time began along with the creature God made." Hence, if He made it, its coming-to-be has gone into the past which is the beginning of time.

Secunda ratio. Item secundo, considerando participationem essendi. Eo[120] enim quo participat esse, non habet esse
plenum, sed contractum et limitatum et quantum ad essentiam
et quantum ad modum.[121] Igitur sicut participat esse finitum,
sic et modum essendi finitum.[122] Sed habere esse sine limitatione[123] dicit modum [L 98d] essendi infinitum. Ergo non [F
62c] convenit[124] habenti esse participatum. Quod dicat talem
modum essendi multipliciter[125] patet: quia excedit omne esse
ex tempore in infinitum. Item,[126] quia secundum hoc, tantum
est suum esse vel tam diuturnum extensive sicut esse divinum
intensive, et tam longa volubilitas temporis quanta simplicitas
aeternitatis; quod est impossibile, sicut invenire mundum tantum quantitate molis sicut Deus est quantitate virtutis. Unde
Augustinus, *De civitate* XI, cap. 5:[127] "Si infinita spatia temporis ante mundum cogitant, in quibus non videtur eis Deus ab
opere cessare potuisse, similiter cogitent extra mundum infinita
spatia locorum," quia idem est iudicium de ante et de extra
mundum. — Quod si dicas non esse simile, quia ponere magnitudinem infinitam est ponere infinitum actu; ponere autem[128]
tempus infinitum non est ponere aliquid[129] actu infinitum, quia
partes temporis non sunt simul; contra: tempus est aliquod ens;
ergo tempus infinitum, ens vel essentia infinita creatae durationis aequans aeternitatem Dei; et si non in simplicitate, tamen in
durationis immensitate a parte ante.

---

[120] From *Eo enim* to *immensitate a parte ante* (i.e., the end of the para-
graph), the text is incorporated by Roger Marston into his *Quodl.* I, q. 1, nn. 9-
10; ed G. F. Eztkorn — I. C. Brady (Quarracchi 1968) 8–9.
[121] modum] essendi *add.* Marston.
[122] Igitur . . . finitum *om.* F.
[123] limitatione F, initio vel principio L. (this sentence is omitted by
Marston).
[124] convenit *om.* F.
[125] multipliciter *om.* L.
[126] Item *om* L.
[127] PL 41, 320; CSEL 40–1, 517, CCL 48, 325.
[128] ponere autem] sed ponere L.
[129] aliquid *om.* L.

Second Reason: In the second place, by considering its participation in being. For by the very fact that it participates in *esse*, it does not have *esse* in its fullness, but rather in a contracted and limited way in terms both of essence and of mode. Consequently, just as it shares finite *esse*, so too its mode of being is finite. But to have *esse* without limitation says an infinite mode of being. Hence, this does not fit a being which has participated *esse*. That it does say such a mode of being is evident from many considerations: (1) because it infinitely surpasses every *esse* created in time; (2) because, according to this, its *esse* endures as long extensively as does the divine *esse* intensively, and the changeableness of time is as long as eternity is simple; but this is impossible, just as it is impossible to find a world whose mass is as great as God's power. In *De civitate* XI, ch. 5, Augustine says: "If they think of infinite expanses of time before the world in which it seems to them that God could have stopped working, in like manner let them think of infinite expanses of space outside of the world," since the same judgment holds for "before" and "outside of" the world. But if you should say that these two are not alike because infinite magnitude posits an actual infinite, while infinite time does not, since the parts of time are not simultaneous, I argue to the contrary that time is some sort of being and is, therefore, an infinite being or an infinite essence of created duration equal to God's infinity. And if it is not equal to God's infinity in its simplicity, still it is equal to it in the immensity of its past duration.

Item, quod modus sit infinitus, probatio: quia infinitas a
parte prima[130] est possibilis quia semper est actu finitum quod
acceptum est et infinitum in potentia tantum. Sed in infinitate a
parte ante est econtra infinitum in actu et in potentia. In actu
inquam,[131] quia tantum habet in actu quantum habet acceptum; et in potentia, ut de futuro dictum est. Haec sententia col-
ligitur ex Augustino, *Super Genesim contra Manichaeum*,
dicente:[132] "Cum ipsa creatura quam fecit Deus tempora esse
coeperunt; et ideo dicuntur aeterna tempora. Non tamen sic
sunt aeterna tempora quomodo aeternus est Deus, quia Deus
est ante tempora, qui fabricator est temporum, sicut omnia
quae fecit Deus bona sunt valde, sed non sic bona sunt quomodo bonus est Deus qui illa fecit." Ergo ex hiis verbis patet quod
sicut bonitas est penitus infinite minor bonitate, ita duratio
duratione.

Tertia ratio. Item, tertio hoc patet ex modo suae originis,
quia est ex nihilo, et ita aliquando non fuit. — Respondetur[133]
quod intelligendum est negative: mundus factus est de nihilo,
hoc est de non-aliquo, ita quod non-esse non[134] praecessit esse
secundum durationem, sed esse mundi nihil praecessit. — Sed
istud improbatur per rationem praetactam,[135] quoniam sicut
versio in non-esse non potest stare cum infinitate a parte post,
ita nec eductio de non-esse cum infinitate a parte ante. Item,
accipere esse non de aliquo dicit maiorem novitatem quam
accipere esse de aliquo, quia quod accipit esse ab aliquo non

---

[130] prima L, ante primo F. (*post* would seem to be called for).
[131] inquam L, nunquam F.
[132] Book I, c. 2, n. 4 (PL 34, 175).
[133] Respondetur] Si respondetur L; cf. St. Thomas, *Summa theol.* I, 46, 2, ad
2 (297b 25–33).
[134] non L, rerum F.
[135] See arg. f, above; and a parallel text in Pecham's *Quodl. Romanum*, q. V.
"Respondeo. Hic implicantur duae difficultates. Una est: An mundus potuit esse
vel creari ab aeterno. Et certum est quod non. Probatur sic: quia habuit esse post
non-esse, id est creatus est de non-aliquo. Sicut igitur impossibile est mundum
durare in infinitum a parte post et tamen verti in nihilum, ita impossibile est
quod fuerit ab aeterno ex parte ante et tamen fuerit eductus de nihilo"; ed. cit.,
16, 16–22.

Further, that its mode of being is infinite is proved thus: infinity in the future is possible because what is grasped is always actually finite and infinite in potency only. But infinity in the past is, on the contrary, infinite both actually and potentially. Actually, I say, because it has in act as much as has been gone through; and potentially from what has been said about the future. This opinion is taken from Augustine in *Super Genesim contra Manichaeum* where he says: "Time began together with the very creature God made and so time is called eternal. Nonetheless time is not eternal in the way in which God is eternal, because God is before time, since He creates it. In the same way all that God made was very good, but it is not for that reason good in the way in which God Who made it is good." From these words, then, it is evident that just as the one goodness is wholly and infinitely less than the other, so is the one duration less than the other.

Third Reason: Again, in the third place, this is evident from the way in which the world began. Since it came from nothing, at one time or another it was not. In reply it is said that this must be understood negatively: the world was made out of nothing, that is, out of not-something, so that *non-esse* did not precede *esse* in duration, but rather nothing preceded the world's *esse*. But this is rejected for the reason already touched upon, namely, that just as a return to *non-esse* is incompatible with an infinite future, so too eduction from *non-esse* is incompatible with an infinite past. Further, to get *esse* not from something says a greater novelty than to get *esse* from something, because what gets *esse* from something is not totally produced but in some respect already was. But if the world has

totaliter producitur, sed secundum aliquid[136] prius fuit. Sed si mundus factus fuisset de aliquo, habuisset esse novum et ex tempore, ut probat Philosophus.[137] Ergo multo magis si habuit esse non de aliquo, habuit esse novum necessario. Damascenus, cap. 8:[138] "Creatio ex Dei voluntate opus exsistens, [L 99a] non coaeterna est cum Deo, quia non aptum natum est quod ex non-ente ad esse deducitur coaeternum esse ei, qui sine principio est et semper est." Et haec est etiam ratio Anselmi, Monologion," 24 cap.[139]

(IV.) Item, hoc patet ex mensura suae productionis, quae est nunc aevi vel nunc temporis. Nunc autem creationis est terminus sui esse a parte ante. Quod autem habet terminum initialem, non habet essendi infinitatem. Ergo si mundus productus est in tempore, productus est in temporis[140] initio. De instanti productionis dicit Hugo, parte prima, cap. 5:[141] "Credimus unum et idem prorsus momentum temporis fuisse, ut in tempore creata sit rerum visibilium corporaliumque materia, [et invisibilium in angelica natura essentia]." [F 62d]

(V.) Item, hoc patet considerando decursum temporis, quoniam[142] revolutio una tardior est quam alia, quia plures praece-

---

[136] aliquid **F**, quid **L**.

[137] *Physic.* VIII, t. 2 and 10, c. I (250b 24: 251b 17).

[138] *De fide orthodoxa* I, c. 8 (PG 94, 814 A–B); versio Burgundionis, c. 8, n. 4 (ed. E. M. Buytaert, St. Bonaventure, N.Y. 1955, 32). Quoted by R. Marston, *Quodl.* I, q. 1, n. 2 (ed. cit., 4); and in part by St. Thomas, *De aeternitate mundi,* n. 10.

[139] Thus St. Anselm writes: "Nam vel hoc solo veram aeternitatem soli illi inesse substantiae, quae sola non facta sed factrix esse inventa est, aperte percipitur; quoniam vera aeternitas principii finisque meta carere intelligitur; quod nulli rerum creatarum convenire, eo ipso quod de nihilo factae sunt, convincitur"; PL 158, 178 A.

[140] temporis *om.* **F**.

[141] PL 176, 189 D; at the end of the citation there is a lacuna in **F** (only) of somewhat over two lines, which we have endeavoured to supply from Hugo's text.

[142] Marston uses *revolutio . . . tale nunquam eveniet* in *Quodl.* I, q. 1, n. 4; ed. cit. 4.

been made out of something, it would have had a new *esse* and that arising in time, as the Philosopher proves. All the more reason, therefore, why, if it has *esse* not from something, it necessarily had a new *esse*. Damascene in ch. 8 says: "Creation, a work whose existence depends on God's will, is not coeternal with God because what is brought down from *non-esse* to *esse* is not by nature apt to be coeternal with Him Who is without beginning and forever." And this is also Anselm's argument in *Monologion*, ch. 24.

(IV) Again, this is evident from the measure of the world's production which is either the now of eternity or the now of time. The now of creation, however, is the terminus of its *esse* in the past. But what has a beginning point does not have an infinity of being. Hence, if the world was made in time, it was made at the beginning of time. In Part I, ch. 5, Hugo says of this instant of production: "We believe there was one and the same moment of time in which the matter of visible and corporeal things was created [and in which the essence of invisible things in the angelic order was also created.]"

(V) Further, this is evident by considering the flow of time, since one revolution is later than another because many more

dunt unam quam aliam, sicut dies crastina[143] tardior est quam
hodierna. Igitur revolutio omnis quam infinitae praecedunt vel
praecesserunt, est infinitae tarditatis. Sed quod est tale, nunquam eveniet. Ergo si mundus infinito tempore duravit,
hodierna vel crastina revolutio nunquam eveniet. Ideo dicit
Augustinus, *De civitate* XII, cap. 15:[144] "Tempus quoniam
mutabilitate transcurrit, aeternitati immutabili non potest esse
coaeternum. Et ita motus quibus tempora peraguntur Creatori
coaeterni esse non possunt."[145]

Dico igitur quod mundus nullo modo capax fuit aeternae
vel interminabilis durationis. Qui autem posuerunt mundum
Deo coaeternum ex falso fundamento ad hoc moti sunt: vel
quia sine mundo Deum credebant esse[146] otiosum; vel quia
imaginati sunt temporis spatium praecessisse mundum; vel
quia non credebant Deum aliquid facere novum nisi voluntate
affectum et per consequens mutatum. Unde Augustinus, XI
De civitate, cap. 4,[147] loquens de ponentibus mundum aeternum dicit: "Dicunt quidem aliquid unde sibi Deum videntur
velut a fortuita temeritate defendere, ne subito illi credatur
venisse in mentem quod nunquam ante venisset, facere
mundum, et accidisse illi voluntatem novam, cum in nullo
omnino sit mutabilis." Quae falsa fundamenta Augustinus
refellit, ut patebit respondendo ad argumenta.

1. Ad primum de diffusione boni et lucis, dicendum quod
duplex est diffusio illius boni et lucis: quaedam est diffusio
boni[148] interior per aeternas emanationes, quaedam exterior
per rerum temporalium[149] productionem. Interior de necessitate est aeterna propter uniformitatem et perfectissimam actu-
alitatem divinae naturae. Secunda autem, quae est temporalium

---

[143] dies crastina] postcrastina L.
[144] Num. 2, or chapter 16 in newer editions (PL 41, 364s; CSEL 40–1, 594,
1–9; CCL 48, 372, 83–92). Augustine's words were cited at great length by St.
Thomas, *De aeternitate mundi*, n. 11.
[145] Lacuna of four lines in F only.
[146] esse *om.* F.
[147] Num. 2 (PL 41, 319; CSEL 40–1, 515; CCL 48, 324).
[148] est diffusio boni *om.* F.
[149] temporalium F, naturalium L.

precede one than the other, just as tomorrow is later than today. Consequently, every revolution which an infinite number of days precedes or has preceded is infinitely later. But something of that sort will never come to pass. If, therefore, the world has lasted through an infinite time, today's or tomorrow's revolution will never come to pass. Hence, Augustine in *De civitate* XII, ch. 15, says: "Since time passes because it is changeable, it cannot be coeternal with immutable eternity. And, in like manner, motion, by which time is driven, cannot be coeternal with the Creator."

I say, therefore, that the world was in no way capable of eternal or endless duration. Those, however, who held on false grounds that the world is coeternal with God were moved to do so either because, without the world, they believed God to be idle, or because they imagined that a space of time preceded the world, or because they did not believe that God makes anything new, unless He is affected by will and consequently changed. So Augustine in *De civitate* XI, ch. 4, speaking about those who hold the world to be eternal, says: "Some say this in order to defend God, as it seems to them, from arbitrary hastiness, as it were, lest it be believed that something suddenly came to His mind which had never occurred to Him before, namely, to create the world, and that He happened to change His will even though He is in no way subject to change." Augustine refuted these false premises as will become evident from the answers to the objections.

1. In reply to the first objection concerning the diffusion of good and of light, it must be said that such diffusion is of two sorts: one is the interior diffusion of good through eternal emanation, the other is exterior through the production of temporal things. The interior diffusion is necessarily eternal because of the uniformity and most perfect actuality of the divine nature. The second, however, which is proper to time and to temporal

et temporalis,[150] de necessitate est secundum quod congruit
creaturae. Unde sicut universum est finitum nec capax infinitatis in magnitudine, ita nec tempus capax erat infinitatis actu-
alis ex aliqua parte, et ideo ipsum, cum sit pars universi, certo
termino et mensura est perventum. Aliter finitum esset suscep-
tivum modi infiniti, ut dictum est. Et quod [L 99b] dicit
Augustinus[151] quod sola bonitas Dei fuit causa istorum, dico
quod verum est, sed non causa defectuum, sicut novitas et vertibilitas et parvitas quae sequuntur creaturam in quantum ex
nihilo. Novitas, quia ab alio facta est; vertibilitas, quia ex[152]
nihilo facta est; parvitas, quia participative facta est.

2. Ad secundum dicendum quod aeternitas soli Deo convenit, nec potest[153] alii convenire, sicut dicit Augustinus, *Super
Genesim* VIII:[154] "Incommutabilis est natura Trinitatis, et ob
hoc ita aeterna ut aliquid ei coaeternum esse non possit."
Quod etiam plures non possunt esse aeternitates[155] probat
Anselmus, *De incarnatione Verbi*, cap. 14.[156] — Tamen aliquando aeternum dicitur largius: sicut super[157] Gen. 3, 22: *Ne
sumat de ligno vitae et comedat et vivat in aeternum*, id est per
magnum spatium temporis, sic ubi[158] Apostolus dicit, II ad
Timoth. I, 9: *Quae data est nobis ante tempora saecularia*, ibi
littera Augustini habet *ante tempora aeterna*. Quod exponit,
Super Genesim contra Manichaeum I, dicens:[159] "Mundus fecit
Deus et cum ipsa creatura quam fecit Deus tempora esse
coeperunt; et ideo dicuntur aeterna tempora." Ergo sensus est:
si ignis fuisset aeternus,[160] hoc est quantumcumque amplius

---

[151] See above, in the first arg. of the present question.
[152] ex F, de L.
[153] potest] fecit F.
[154] *De Genesi ad litteram* VIII, c. 23, n. 44 (PL 34, 389; CSEL 28-1, 262).
[155] aeternitates] trinitates F.
[156] PL 178, 282 B.
[157] super *om.* F.
[158] ubi] hic F.
[159] Chapt. 2, n. 3 (PL 34, 175)
[160] See the words of Augustine in the second argument.

things, is necessarily according to the nature of a creature. Consequently, just as the universe is finite and is incapable of infinite magnitude, so too time was incapable of an actual infinity of past or future, and so time itself, since it is part of the universe, is bounded by a definite limit and measure. Otherwise, what is finite would be capable of an infinite mode, as was said above. And as Augustine says, only the goodness of God was the cause of such things; I say that this is true, but it [God's goodness] is not the cause of their defects, such as their newness and changeableness and smallness, all of which are true of a creature insofar as it comes from nothing: newness because it is made by another; changeableness because it is made from nothing; smallness because it is made according to participation.

2. Reply to the second objection: eternity is proper to God alone and cannot be proper to anything else, as Augustine says in *Super Genesim* VIII: "The nature of the Trinity is totally unchangeable, and for that reason it is so eternal that nothing else can be coeternal with it." Again, in *De incarnatione Verbi*, ch. 14, Anselm proves that there cannot be many eternities. Nonetheless sometimes a thing is said to be eternal in a broader sense, for example, Gen. 3:22: "Lest he take from the tree of life and eat and live eternally," i.e., for a long period of time, and so too where the Apostle says, II Tim. 1:9: "Which was given to us before time immemorial." Augustine's text reads "from time eternal." In *Super Genesim contra Manichaeum* I, he explains this: "God made the world, and time began along with the creature God made; and therefore it is called eternal time." The sense, therefore, is: if fire were eternal, that is to say, however much more the fire would have been than in fact it

fuisset quam fuit, vel si fuisset in principio ipso¹⁶¹ temporis in specie distinctus. Quodsi dicatur aeternum Deo coaevum, implicatio est oppositorum, quia ponit accidens infinitum in subiecto finito, et sequitur ut splendor esse aeternus, sicut posito impossibili sequitur quod impossibili implicatur. Et sic dicendum de vestigio [F 63a] pedis in pulvere rationibus consimilibus.

3. Ad tertium dicendum quod 'tota ratio facti est potentia facientis'. Sed tamen defectibilitas sequitur creaturam in quantum ex nihilo est, cuius causa Deus non est. — Item, cum dico posse rei creabilis, licet nihil dicam positive nisi potentiam Creatoris, dico tamen cum hoc privationem prohibitionis¹⁶² sui esse. Quaedam enim prohibent suum esse, ut omnia in quorum intellectu negatio clauditur. Licet igitur creabile non dicat potentiam aliam a potentia Creatoris, tamen excludit impedimentum, quia termini non repugnant.

4. Ad quartum dicendum quod non est impossibilitas¹⁶³ a pari ad utrumque, quia in eo quod est 'creaturam esse aeternam' opposita clauduntur, non autem in eo quod est 'creaturam creari'.

5. Ad quintum dicendum quod plus potest Deus de nihilo in eo quod posse est posse, sed hoc posse non est posse.

6–7. Ad sextum dicendum quod illud argumentum procedit ex falsa imaginatione, quasi Deus spatio mundum praecessit. Amplius, dico quod Deus nihil potest velle nisi secundum leges sapientiae. Ideo non potest velle aliquid infinitum inesse subiecto finito.¹⁶⁴ — Et sic patet ad septimum.¹⁶⁵

---

¹⁶¹ in principio ipso F, a principio L.
¹⁶² prohibitionis] probationis F.
¹⁶³ impossibilitas] argumentum L.
¹⁶⁴ In the margin of F at this point there is one note deleted and partly covered by another (at third hand?), which is quite illegible; it seems to refer to the lack of a response to the seventh argument.
¹⁶⁵ septimum] sextum.

was, or [it means] if fire in the very beginning of time were of a different kind. But if "eternal" is taken as "coeval with God," opposites are implied, since this posits an infinite accident in a finite subject, and it follows that its splendor would be eternal just as it follows that once an impossibile supposition has been granted, the impossible is implied. The arguments about footprints in the dust are answered in a similar way.

3. Reply to the third objection, namely, "the whole explanation of what is made is in the maker." Nevertheless defectibility is a property of the creature insofar as it comes from nothing. God does not cause this defectibility. Again, when I say the "to be able to be created" of a thing, although I say nothing positive except the Creator's power, still I connote the absence of an impediment to its *esse*. For some things do impede *esse*, for example, everything in the understanding of which there is a hidden negation. Hence, although "to be able to be created" does not say any potency except the Creator's, still it excludes any obstacle, since the terms are not contradictory.

4. Reply to the fourth objection: the impossibility is not the same in each case because in the phrase "the creature is eternal" contraries are hidden, while this is not so in the phrase "the creature is created."

5. Reply to the fifth objection: God can make more out of nothing in the case where the "possible" is possible, but the "possible" in question is not possible.

6–7. Reply to the sixth and seventh objections: that argument proceeds from a faulty imagination as if God preceded the world in space. Further, I say that God can will nothing except according to the laws of wisdom. And so He cannot will that something infinite inhere in a finite subject. Thus the reply to the seventh objection is evident.

8. Ad octavum[166] dico quod verum est ex parte sui pro tanto quod non procedit ex impotentia quod non producit; sed tamen non congruit omnino potentiae suae.

9. Ad aliud dicendum quod aequipotens est producere finitum sicut infinitum, sed non simul finitum et infinitum.[167]

11. Ad undecimum dicendum[168] quod non est simile de creatione quae terminatur ad esse, et ideo potest habere mensuram; et de versione [L 99c] terminatur ad non-esse, et, quia est defectio, ideo nulla sibi respondet mensura; sed ipsum esse habet ultimum instans sui esse cui nihil succedit nisi non-esse.

---

[166] octavum] vii L.
[167] A marginal note in **F**: Hic autem (?) deest decimi solutio.
[168] undecimum dicendum **F**, aliud **L**.

8. Reply to the eighth objection: it is true of it to the extent that what it does not produce is not produced because of an incapacity; but nonetheless this does not completely square with His power.

9. Reply to the ninth objection: God is equally able to produce something finite and something infinite, but not something both finite and infinite.

11. Reply to the eleventh objection: there is no similarity between creation, which terminates in *esse* and so can have a measure, and destruction which terminates in *non-esse* and so, because it is a defect, has no measure; but *esse* itself has a last instant of its *esse* upon which nothing but *non-esse* follows.